A POETICS OF AUGUSTAN ELEGY: STUDIES OF POEMS BY DRYDEN, POPE, PRIOR, SWIFT, GRAY, AND JOHNSON

by

DONALD C. MELL

RODOPI N.V.

AMSTERDAM 1974

©Editions Rodopi N.V., Amsterdam
Printed in the Netherlands
ISBN: 90–6203–278–8

For my parents

TABLE OF CONTENTS

Preface

For both historical and cultural reasons the English Augustans possessed an acute sense of art and were fascinated by literary artifice whether in the literature of classical Greece and Rome, in the cadences of Scripture, or in the works of their own predecessors. Yet they reveal again and again in their works a sober consciousness of the moral function of literature and its relation to the actual. One happy result of the continuing revaluation of Augustan literature over the past three decades has been to show the crucial importance of rhetorical and stylistic practices to the meaning and purpose of the literature of the period. My approach to Augustan elegy continues this tradition by focusing on the elegist's treatment in his imagination and art of the facts of time and death.

In this study I have attempted to keep my eye on the literary object, and have tried to observe Northrop Frye's prescription for good "academic criticism": that it be "systematic" and that its approach be "categorical" and "descriptive," and that its whole purpose be "to *identify* a writer's work."[1] These following chapters may be read as independent, self-sufficient analyses of the respective elegies. But they more properly constitute what in musical composition is called variations on a theme, the theme in this particular case being the conflicts between art and nature, literature and life, permanence and time at the heart of the Augustan elegiac mode.

Portions of Chapters 2, 3, 5, 6,and 7 have appeared in somewhat different form in *Enlightenment Essays, Modern Language Quarterly, Concerning Poetry, Papers on Language and Literature,* and *Genre* respectively. These essays have been revised for the purpose of this study. I wish to thank the editors of the above journals for their permission to print these materials.

I am grateful for the help provided by the Committees on

1. "Literary Criticism," in *The Aims and Methods of Scholarship in Modern Languages and Literatures,* ed. James Thorpe (New York: Modern Language Association of America, 1963), p. 61.

Faculty Research at Middlebury College and at the University of Delaware in the form of grants which aided in the preparation of this manuscript.

My personal thanks extend to many teachers, colleagues, and friends both in and out of the academic profession. Maurice Johnson, Arthur Scouten, and Clyde Ryals have made a number of helpful suggestions about the manuscript. I also want to thank Ricardo Quintana for his excellent recommendations on Swift and other eighteenth-century matters. Louis L. Martz has been a constant source of inspiration and encouragement over the years, and I wish to acknowledge his good counsel on things literary. My special thanks also to Thomas Van Laan, Richard Francis, George Bahlke, Jay Halio, and Robert Pack for reading sections of the manuscript and providing indispensable advice. Betty Sherman's expert typing and editorial suggestions have helped expedite the manuscript, and Robert Deitz's proofreading has been hopefully foolproof. Margaret Pyle Hassert helped with the index, and I appreciate her efforts.

Chapter One

Except, perhaps, for Gray's *Elegy* the eighteenth century would hardly seem an appropriate place in literary history to find memorable elegiac poetry. Of course, one finds an abundance of self-indulgent graveyard musings on the course of history and civilizations, and this phenomenon should not be surprising in an age given to a poetry of "sensibility" and literature of the "sublime." But if the search takes one to the Augustan or neo-classical writers, a different sensibility is encountered, demonstrating a realistic if sober attitude toward the facts of time, change, and mortality, and a tough-minded assessment of the adequacy of art and artist in coping with these actualities.

Even though our most astute critics of the period have identified strong elegiac strains in the brilliant satiric art of Dryden, Swift, Pope, and Johnson, the formal Augustan elegy that restricts itself to lamenting the death of a specific individual, real or fictional, while praising his life and works, seems devoid of the powerful and deeply felt emotions we associate with great elegiac poetry. In fact, even a cursory glance through English and American poetry shows conclusively that the great elegies of the language are really poems that treat the death of an individual as a pretext for philosophical probings into such topics as the nature of divine justice, the alienation of the artist, the existence of God, the viability of an art form, the transforming power of the imagination — all questions which have perplexed man as artist from his origins. These "big" elegies of Chaucer, Donne, Milton, Shelley, Tennyson, Arnold, Whitman, or even W. H. Auden are expansive in manner and comprehensive if circumspect in their analysis of the irrevocable facts of time and mortality, and often end up defining the intellectual matrix of their respective ages, rather than expressing regret over personal and artistic loss.

This is not the Augustan elegiac mode, which, in the words of a trusted critic, gives "a truly honest appraisal of life and the poet's part in it ... made only in the uncompromising light of the facts of mortality."[1] A good deal is known and has been written about this "honest" and "uncompromising" acceptance of the human situation as the theme of Augustan poetry, and the correlative view of life's brevity and time's inevitable passing. The world of the Augustan is surely one of limits, restrictions, in which life is circumscribed by doubts and skepticism, and all human faculties are irremediably flawed and suspect. And this outlook is expressed sharply through the characteristic irony of the age. Augustan elegy reflects, among other things, an awareness of this limited nature of human life and relationships. Even allowing for some irony, it is the ethos informing the highest tribute Swift imagined his closest friends, colleagues, and supporters would pay at his death:

> Poor POPE will grieve a Month; and GAY
> A Week; and ARBUTHNOTT a Day.

Such a grudging compliment does not encourage expectations of elegy delving into the profound mysteries of life or death!

Augustan elegy tends to restrict itself in the sense that it stays close to the occasion, actual or fictional as the case may be, giving rise to the poem itself. Thus we seldom lose sight of the person or persons being praised and mourned. But it is also close to the occasion in still another, more important way; for its *real* subject, transcending all others, is ultimately the question of its own significance and meaning in a world of time and death. In Augustan elegy the poem is its own subject and also the language or medium through which that subject is not only rendered but scrutinized. We are, therefore, as fully conscious of its contrived nature and verbal calculation as we are of its sincerity and heartfelt emotion.

But the Augustan elegist is truly self-expressive, as radically so as any poet of the romantic era when self-expression was supposedly invented. Concern for his language and art is a poet's central professional interest as well as a most personal and private matter. It is essentially his only way of speaking about and dealing with the reality around him. One possible explanation for this emphasis in Augustan elegy is the highly "professional" character of most Augustan writers from Dryden to Johnson. A true profes-

---

1. Rachel Trickett, *The Honest Muse: A Study in Augustan Verse* (Oxford: Clarendon Press, 1967), p. 24.

sional makes no bones about the importance he attaches to his profession, even when he seemingly deprecates his own enthusiasms, as, for example, Swift and Pope often do. Such posturing is, of course, intimately part of the game of art. But as a professional, a writer constantly analyzes and evaluates the significance and limitations of his art as valid representation of reality, and in the process formally orders his experiences of time and loss which call into question these intimations of order and the idea of permanence through art.

The differences among the poems chosen for this study have been widely noted, but they exist in stylistic accidentals and in the poet's individualized habits of expression. Rebecca Price Parkin has interestingly discussed with a "historiographic purpose" the Oldham and Levet elegies, for example, asserting that they "function as microcosmic reflectors of a complex and still controversial shift in sensibility."[2] The shift she refers to is from a kind of literary neoclassicism of "pure, unblended Romanism" in Dryden to a Christianized, humanized, and personalized brand of neoclassicism in Johnson.

Whatever the value of using a poem or poems to illustrate changing patterns of literary or intellectual history, such an approach tends to ignore continuities and shared qualities in these Augustan elegies, and, more importantly, blurs the significance of elegy as aesthetic construct in the continuum of time and process. The elegist's self-consciousness about the function of art is implicit in the nature of elegy itself, whose genesis is peculiarly the poet's personal response to loss and time. All the poems chosen for this study are basically concerned with the adequacy of art as a defense against time and change. Swift's, Pope's, and Gray's openly address themselves to the problem; Dryden's, Prior's, and Johnson's are more oblique, demonstrating by the very creative act which produces them the value of imaginative idealization. At the same time, however, the inspiration for elegy is a tacit acknowledgment of the unbridgeable gulf between art and life.

Of course, this theme is not uniquely Augustan, nor is it an exclusive feature of the Augustan elegiac mode, as this study tries

2. The Journey Down the Great Scale Reflected in Two Neoclassical Elegies," *Enlightenment Essays,* 1 (1970), 197.

to indicate through selective comparison with elegies of other literary ages. Indeed, the highly stylized products of contemporary novelists like Nabokov, Barth, or Mailer, to name only three, alert us to the artists' continuing concern for a literary mode of existence never entirely identical with or separate from our experience of reality. Yeats was right when he incisively defined the true nature of all art, while defending his own play: "for the imagination and intellect are that which is eternal in man crying out against that which is temporal and perishing."[2a] If not exactly "crying out" in Yeats's sense, the elegist is attempting to rescue reality from time by proclaiming his subject's life and significance through art.

But if these elegiac tensions between art and time are not exclusively Augustan, the Augustan elegist does structure his imaginative idealizations and experience of time in a distinctive way. The distinction of this mode relates to the metaphor of "miniaturization." Philip Stevick has noted the importance of smallness in eighteenth-century literature, despite the attention paid to "representations of spaciousness," epic grandeur and grandiloquence. For Stevick, "miniaturization" entails "construction of a model, with the essential features intact, of a larger entity."[3] But this "larger entity" is a complex affair: the small implies the large at the same time the mighty and grand are scaled down to the miniature. Past and present exist in a double vision which gives a comprehensive view of man's nature. We enjoy the jolt received while experiencing the mock-heroic mode, for instance, in which unimportant situations or events are treated in exalted terms for the purpose of reduction and devaluation, laughter and ridicule. But the poetic action informing the mock-heroic mode can enhance as well as subvert. Pope enlarges to reduce in the *Rape of the Lock,* while also suggesting that the heroic spirit is somehow metamorphosed in the forms and ceremonies of Belinda's world. In the *Dunciad,* however, Pope's readers are terrified by the grotesque and frightening implications of duncery for civilization itself.

2a *The Letters of W. B. Yeats,* ed. Allan Wade (New York: Macmillan, 1955), p. 310.

3. "Miniaturization in Eighteenth-Century English Literature," *UTQ,* 38 (1969), 159, 161.

The heroic couplet can easily serve as another useful example of Augustan "miniaturization." Its uniqueness as a rhetorical device exists in the fact of its compression and brevity. Using the attributes of prose discourse, the skillful satirist creates through his couplet the rich suggestiveness peculiar to poetic effect. The restrictions and limitations built into the device are not reductive, regressive, nor do they interfere in any way with the function of satire in ridiculing vice and folly. In fact, the compression itself helps to generate the most complex meanings by forcing the familiar into incongruous and therefore provocative circumstances.

A similar complexity is characteristic of Augustan elegy, especially in the poems chosen for this study. These poems, even Swift's, are essentially compressed, concentrated, and predictable in their basic elegiac action and design. The metaphor of "miniaturization" operates to create the widest possible significance and range of feeling commensurate with the Augustan sensibility. "Models" of a peculiar Augustan consciousness of time and change these poems may be, but they also constantly push outward to the "larger entities" and fundamental relationships between art and life.

These elegies are also self-consciously conventional in feeling and thought, and reflect traditional elegiac procedures. In their traditional elegiac function and conventionality, they can be compared to pastoral, another form of literary "miniaturization." The combination of predictable elegiac action and the reduction into small scale of complex human emotions is, as in pastoral, the "process of putting the complex into the simple," in Empson's words. But the simplicities and idealized relationships of pastoral are never an adequate substitute for flesh-and-blood reality, and such idealizations and simplifications are indeed meaningless if cut off from the contrasting actualities of experience, as every pastoralist acknowledges.

Limited in scope and given to artifice and the restrictions of formal structure, these poems might appear to be merely pedestrian examples of the so-called Augustan sensibility. But as in the best Augustan verse a complex simplicity obtains. These elegies focus complicated issues by particularizing and universalizing simultaneously, and in the process generate a wealth of implication and meaning beyond their immediate occasions. T. S. Eliot's point about Dryden's verse is appropriate here: these Augustan elegies, like Dryden's poetic language, "state immensely."

Chapter Two

Recent studies of Augustan pastoral poetry have emphasized the idea of the imagination as an idealizing power by which the poet transforms the fallen world of experience into a timeless world of order, form, and beauty. Martin Battestin, for example, describes the "intellectual impetus" behind Augustan pastoral art as a preoccupation with "the nature, the mystery, the efficacy of Art itself, viewed in relation to those correlative concepts with which the artist is most nearly concerned: the meaning of Time and Nature in a fallen world."[1]

But this pastoral mode is strongly dependent on elegiac feelings, for the nostalgic impulse behind creation of an uncomplicated, pure, and all-harmonious world of pastoral is fundamentally the human experience of time and mortality — the explicit subject matter of elegy. This conflation of both ideal and real perhaps accounts for the continuous presence and popularity of pastoral elegy throughout literary history. Like pastoral, elegy is "literary," highly artificial in style and conventional in feeling and form; and, like pastoral, it is the result not only of man's recognition of the facts of time and death, but of his desire to compensate through art for this fact of mortality. For both modes, however, crisis in love or disaster in death paradoxically leads to a new creation or renewal of life, through art. But it is explicitly in elegy that the idealizations of art and fictions of the imagination are scrutinized against the inescapable actualities of experience.

The important feature of Augustan elegy is its treatment of death as a fact or absolute of life. But this realistic assessment of man's limitations is always accomplished through the instrument of art, paradoxically denying the very motive for and theme of elegy itself. Inevitably, the elegist's concern for the achievements of the dead indirectly becomes an exploration of the nature and

1. "The Transforming Power — Nature and Art in Pope's Pastorals," *ECS*, 2 (1969), 189, 190; see also "Menalcas' Song: The Meaning of Art and Artifice in Gay's Poetry," *JEGP*, 65 (1966), 662 -679.

function of art as an adequate defense against time. The solution is never "romantic," as when the oppositions between art and life are reconciled in a transcendental symbol such as a Grecian urn or a metal bird of Byzantium; nor is the solution "Christian" or "religious," as when the oppositions are transformed by an outside force like Christ, as often experienced in Renaissance elegy. The Augustan elegist's solution is unique: these conflicting elegiac oppositions are presented objectively through the permanence of form and the ideality of art.

The elegist, moreover, seeks to dramatize the tensions between the imaginative ideal and flesh-and-blood reality by seeking to reconcile these oppositions through the creation of order and form, life and permanence in the very act of elegizing. This condition of art is the poet's way of containing, composing, and finally coping with time and mortality. As Allen Tate has nicely put it in reference to the poems of John Crowe Ransom, the supreme twentieth-century elegist: "Our mastery of decay and death is in the ironic cultivation of 'grave rites and funerals.' "[2] In its creative function, then, the elegiac imagination mediates between the ideal and the real.

In some poems Dryden directly, if conventionally, affirms the power of art over time:

> For ev'n when Death dissolves our Humane Frame,
> The Soul returns to Heav'n, from whence it came;
> Earth keeps the Body, Verse preserves the Fame.[3]
>
> ("To My Honour'd Kinsman
> John Driden," 207-209)

A more radical claim for art's transforming power is voiced in another elegy:

> As Earth thy Body keeps, thy Soul the Sky,
> So shall this Verse preserve thy Memory;
> For thou shalt make it live, because it sings of thee.
>
> ("Eleanora," 375-77)

In both examples, the triplet construction underscores the finality

---

2. "Gentleman in a Dustcoat," Kenyon College *Alumni Bulletin,* 26, No. 2 (1968), 33.

3. *The Poems of John Dryden,* ed. James Kinsley, 4 Vols. (Oxford: Clarendon Press, 1958); all quotations of Dryden are from this edition.

of death at the same time it lends weight to the idea that art somehow rescues reality from time.

Dryden's famous elegy "To the Memory of Mr. Oldham" (1694) addresses itself to these elegiac oppositions through devices of allusion, imagery and symbol. The poem is familiarly described as "moving," "noble," "perfectly proportioned," devoid of "commotion," and exhibiting "the satisfying completeness of the statement."[3a] As archetypal representation of neo-classical decorum and poetic craftmanship, the poem might seem free of the tensions and ambiguities inherent in the Augustan elegiac mode. But the contrary is true: first, John Oldham's poetry is a mirror which reflects Dryden's own artistic concerns; second, the poem embodies rather than expresses directly the above-mentioned opposition between art and the experience of time; and third, its theme is finally the nature and function of that art. Dryden commemorates his fellow satirist and laments his untimely death, while simultaneously focusing on his own role as imaginative artist, exploring the nature of art's power as he acknowledges its limitations as consolation for mortality.

In his tribute to Oldham, Dryden faced a problem of tone: that is, the possibility of sounding either self-abasing or simply self-satisfied, a danger his predecessor in classical elegy, Ben Jonson, did not encounter when lamenting the death of the far greater Shakespeare. Dryden solved this problem, as he never seems quite able to do in his panegyrics and dedicatory essays, much as Milton solved a similar one in writing about Edward King.[4] By treating

3a. Cf. John R. Clark, " 'To the Memory of Mr. Oldham': Dryden's Disquieting Lines," *CP*, 3 (1970), 43 -49. In a strong dissent from received opinion on the poem, Clark contends that, read as elegy, the poem has been "second-guessed" and that it moves not to resolution, acceptance, and consolation, as in traditional elegiac action, but away from the "masks of rhetoric and metaphor" to the speaker's direct confrontation with the "disturbing fact of death itself" (pp. 47, 46). What Clark in reality says is that for Dryden fear shatters artistic illusion and feeling takes precedence over form. I fully agree with the statement that "the poem is concertedly about the speaker 'Dryden' " (p. 47), yet given the allusiveness of the concluding lines, the poem surely does not move from literature to life but to life *through* literature. Paradoxically, for Dryden generally the more "literary" the poem the more intense and personal it becomes.

4. For a brief but helpful comparison of mostly superficial likenesses and

King's death in a pastoral setting, Milton depersonalizes emotion paradoxically to expand the poem's significance for him as a young, dedicated poet. Dryden's strategy is peculiarly Augustan in "To Mr. Oldham," accomplishing depersonalization through allusion which relates Oldham to figures of classical literature and history. Earl Wasserman has rightly warned us against minimizing the scope of Pope's classical reference by considering simply the text of his allusions without recognizing the fuller context they can introduce into his poems.[5] In "To Mr. Oldham" Dryden's allusions function in a comparable way.

The allusion to the famous footrace between Nisus and Euryalus in Book V of Virgil's *Aeneid* establishes an epic context for the fictional relationship between the two satirists set forth in the first ten lines of the elegy. The two men are at once close and remote, alike and different, young and old, living and dead, brothers in the writing of satire, yet differentiated by separate fates. This series of oppositions is fully dramatized by the reversal of expectations in line 8: "The last set out the soonest did arrive." Dryden conveniently edits out the second challenger (Salius) in the episode to highlight the paradoxical rivalry and friendship motifs for the Oldham elegy.

The continuation of the Nisus-Euryalus episode in *Aeneid,* Book IX, further de-emphasizes the rivalry motif while stressing the ideas of friendship and impending death, all relevant themes of Dryden's poem. In this particular portion of the account, published, as was that of the famous race, one year after the elegy as a dry run on his final versions in the complete *Aeneid* (1697), Dryden was to emphasize qualities of mutuality and corporateness which characterize the relationship the elegy develops between the speaker and Oldham as the mythic combatants in warfare of wit of lines 1-10:

> One was their friendship, their desire was one;
> With minds united in the field they warr'd,
> And now were both by choice upon the guard.
> *(Aeneis,* IX, 113-115; version in *Sylvae*)

differences between the two elegies, see Bruce King, " 'Lycidas' and 'Oldham,' " *Etudes Anglaises,* T. 19 (1966), 60 -63.

5. "The Limits of Allusion in 'The Rape of the Lock' " *JEGP,* 65 (1966), 425.

The formal elevation here transforms their fate of inevitable death into heroic terms, adding a note of dignity and tragedy to the coming sacrifice. When translated into an elegiac context, however, death looms as the irreversible fact of existence. Through allusion, then, Dryden beautifully blends elegiac with heroic tones.

The allusion applies to Dryden's elegy in still other ways. The idea of a "race" suggests both mutual dedication and competitiveness. But it also introduces the most conventional of elegiac motifs, repeated again and again in poems as diverse, say, as Wordsworth's "Three Years She Grew" or Housman's "To an Athlete Dying Young" — the race against time. These antithetical motivations are expressed through explicit Virgilian fictions. The Nisus-Euryalus episode has been called an "*exemplum* of friendship,"[6] but more important is the mythologizing of this friendship and competition as a race against time that cannot be won, except in the reader's capacity to recreate the moment imaginatively, and therefore to affirm the power of art to counteract the effects of time. By rendering thought and feeling, by alluding to Virgil, Dryden avoids the distracting intrusion of actual biography. In this poetic world elegiac emotions are formalized and distanced, freed of the personal and topical, and given symbolic form in Dryden's artifact.

Yet the speaker's simultaneous engagement with and detachment from actuality does not fully exclude thoughts of death. Form allows us to contain emotion but not to avoid the facts of change, loss, and death. Indeed, the actual experience of time gives rise to the artful mastery of time through form. Death mythologized softens the reality, but such generalizing cannot adequately compensate for the reality of the loss which the poem laments. The speaker's dual role as participant in the race as well as artist employing allusion to mediate between myth and actual experience symbolizes the elegiac tensions between art and life at the heart of Augustan elegy.

Another significant classical allusion — this one referring to the two Marcelluses, one Augustus's promising nephew early dead, the other the Roman general of the Second Punic War — further complicates the elegiac conflicts between mutability and perman-

6. Arthur W. Hoffman, *John Dryden's Imagery* (Gainesville: University of Florida Press, 1962), p. 93.

ence, the real and the ideal, life and art. Virgil's treatment of the two historical figures of classical antiquity constitutes a single identity: a glorious general of Roman history is fused with a "godlike youth," who, except for "fate's severe decree," could emulate the general and also become the "new Marcellus."[7] As in the allusion to Nisus and Euryalus, the oppositions between youth and age, successful competitor and unsuccessful one, glory and sadness, life and death, provide familiar elegiac conflicts.

In both the episode from Dryden's *Aeneid* and in the elegy, death is treated as final and relentless, and this finality may explain why at least one critic has felt that the poem contains no consolation or hope, no sign of accommodation with or acceptance of the facts of time and death.[8] In his visit to the underworld, Aeneas hears his father, Anchises, praise the young Marcellus:

> All gaze, and all admire, and raise a shouting sound:
> But hov'ring Mists around his Brows are spread,
> And Night, with sable Shades, involves his Head.
>
> (*Aeneis*, VI, 1197-1199)

The meaning of the lines and the dramatic emphasis create a mood of uncompromising pathos and an almost stoic acceptance of mortality.

But the fuller context of the reference provides a countermovement to this supposedly somber finale. At the bleakest moment of Anchises' lament for the young Marcellus, we are suddenly aware of feeling being formalized in the language and rhythms of conventional tribute, providing through style, then, the consolation of ritualistic action:

> Ah, cou'dst thou break through Fates severe Decree,
> A new *Marcellus* shall arise in thee!
> Full Canisters of fragrant Lillies bring,

7. If, as Hoffman suggests (p. 96), we view Oldham as a combination of the two Virgilian Marcelluses we witness what could be called a double refracted allusion which further generalizes the conflicting elegiac emotions. For the scene is interpreted for Aeneas by Anchises, the shaping artist in this case, just as future prophecy is in itself a literary convention through which Virgil shapes his total epic vision.

8. See Rachel Trickett, *The Honest Muse: A Study in Augustan Verse* (Oxford: Clarendon Press, 1967), pp. 23, 24.

Mix'd with Purple Roses of the Spring;
Let me with Fun'ral Flow'rs his Body strow;
This Gift which Parents to their Children owe,
This unavailing Gift, at least I may bestow!

(*Aeneis,* VI, 1220-1226)

Speaking in this manner is perhaps Anchises' only defense against time, but the highly ceremonial, public, and conventional rendering of a traditional symbolic action reinforces the ritual movement depicted within the lines: the strewing of the bier with floral tribute.

Dryden's ending of "To Mr. Oldham" is equally conventional and stylized:

Once more, hail and farewel; farewel thou young
But ah too short, *Marcellus* of our Tongue;
Thy Brows with Ivy, and with Laurels bound;
But Fate and gloomy Night encompass thee around. (22-25)

More than a decade before his *Aeneid,* then, Dryden was consciously employing a highly stylized manner of expression when depicting public events such as burial of the dead. The traditional ivy and laurel, emblematic of pastoral art as well as military heroism, appear significantly both in the elegy and in the *Aeneid.* Whether in a pastoral or heroic context, ritual activity is affirmed through stylized diction and predictable idioms. As with the Nisus-Euryalus episode, these allusions constitute Dryden's art of elegiac praise and honor for the dead.[9] The traditional funeral

9. Cf. R. G. Peterson, "The Unavailing Gift: Dryden's Roman Farewell to Mr. Oldham," *MP,* 65 (1969), 235. Peterson quarrels with the term "elegy" to describe the poem, suggesting that Dryden utilized a more limited conventional form: the Roman *conclamatio.* For uses of the classic formula Ave atque Vale, hail and farewell, see Eurydice's cry of despair as Orpheus looks back for her:

And now farewel, involv'd in Shades of Night,
For ever I am ravish'd from thy sight.

(*Georgics,* IV, 718-719)

Or Aeneas's words at the grave of Pallas:

Peace with the *Manes* of great *Pallas* dwell!
Hail, holy Relics, and a last farewell!

(*Aeneis,* XI, 145-146)

Also the final line of Catullus' elegy 101.

games, which provide the original setting for the footrace in "To Mr. Oldham," and the conferring of emblems of victory and defeat by time are commemorative celebrations closely associated with epic poetry and the epic version of reality. In the Oldham elegy, epic associations are miniaturized by Dryden's own elegiac version of reality. Like the epic, elegy is part of a well-established literary tradition, and this tradition operates continuously upon the elegist's consciousness to give his individual feelings intelligible shape. To lament the dead Oldham is, for Dryden, to create a living poetic memorial. The creative act itself reflects the poet's attempt to escape from temporality into permanence.

Another way Dryden explores these conflicting elegiac motifs is through the literary criticism implicit in the poem. It is abundantly clear that this elegy, which purports to praise Oldham's accomplishments, also qualifies the praise through wit and irony. One method of expressing this form of qualified praise is in images of natural process. By utilizing natural imagery, the poet underscores the theme of time through processes of growth and fruition, the passing of seasons, and the cycles of nature.

By means of a rhetorical question (or assertion), Dryden turns Oldham's early and therefore unnatural death into a positive affirmation of his own poetic talent and permanence:[10]

> O early ripe! to thy abundant store
> What could advancing Age have added more? (11-12)

At the same time reminders of time and loss occur in these lines. "Early," "ripe," "advancing age," and "added more" presume natural process through a continuum of time. The timelessness of Oldham's art is asserted, but paradoxically, through images of temporality.

The second appearance of the fruit imagery develops further the interplay between art and time by extending the critique of Oldham's satirical practices:

> Thy generous fruits, though gather'd ere their prime
> Still shew'd a quickness; and maturing time
> But mellows what we write to the dull sweets of Rime. (19-21)

Oldham's "early ripeness" and abundance have become "generous

---

10. Cf. Alan Roper, *Dryden's Poetic Kingdoms* (London: Routledge and Kegan Paul, 1965), p. 46.

fruits" without the characteristic blandness of mature fruit. Old-ham's satires are many, but they retain their own characteristic sharpness ("quickness"). Here, as before with the fruit imagery, the critical commentary is circumscribed by the general elegiac context, with all terms referring – almost in the Keatsian manner of "To Autumn" and with the same ominous quality felt in Keats's ode – to the cycles of growing, maturing, and gathering, to life, vitality, "quickness," and thus to the irrecoverable processes of time, change, and therefore death. These negative features of time are opposed by positive feelings of satisfaction and accomplishment which are the result of process within time. From cyclical renewal arises the only true permanence, in nature as well as art. This organic vitality which characterizes the true order of art derives from the stable world of nature's perpetual returnings.

The last line and a half of the triplet operates as a mild rebuke to the fictional "we" of the poem – the speaker with his controlled and assured voice of experience and his implied audience who "agrees" with the implicit literary judgments. But this "rebuke" to the speaker and his fellow satirists who live on is another in a series of ironic qualifications associated with the seasonal metaphor and the hypothetical reply of "nothing" made to the rhetorical question following the first appearance of the fruit imagery. "What could advancing Age have added more? " says the speaker:

> It might (what Nature never gives the young)
> Have taught the numbers of thy native Tongue.
> But Satyr needs not those, and Wit will shine
> Through the harsh cadence of a rugged line. (13-16)

Yet even though a strong case is made in these lines for the effectiveness of Oldham's youtful satiric excesses, a qualifying framework restrains and controls the praise. Double ironies are operative here because the implied "answer" to the rhetorical question is an unfavorable one, and the negative response is clearly meant to be high praise. "Maturity has its rights," as Paul Ramsey points out, and the whole poem, he rightly insists, contradicts these assertions of harshness as necessarily a "noble error."[11] And

11. *The Art of John Dryden* (Lexington: University of Kentucky Press, 1969), p. 18.

Dryden surely demonstrates his own superior achievement in the following verse: "and Wit will shine / Through the harsh cadence of a rugged line." The metrical roughness, harshness of cadence, and the generally discordant sound, deliberately feigned to demonstrate Oldham's most characteristic manner, reflect the speaker's consciousness of his own smoothness of "numbers" expressed paradoxically in the rough versification typical of the lamented satirist. More important, however, the critical truth is here shown to be the result of artistic allusion. By expressing as well as self-consciously enacting both Oldham's poetic limitations and abilities, Dryden is doing, in Arthur W. Hoffman's words, "the kinds of things poets care about, and they are done not only as part of talking about Oldham but also *for* Oldham."[11a]

Dryden's speaker avoids the charge of condescension or self-righteousness by extending the contrary implications of these critical/laudatory attitudes in the next couplet:

> A noble Error, and but seldom made,
> When Poets are by too much force betray'd. (17-18)

With a trace of his own brand of heroicizing mixed with the pointed irony of the word "seldom," the speaker both exclaims boldly in praise of Oldham's strong feelings and unpolished directness at the same time he qualifies his praise. The "noble Error" is at least not habitual. The word "betray'd" implies a form of artistic violence in sharp contrast to the speaker's urbanity, civility, and controlled literary style. This brief reference to disorder is otherwise balanced by the praiseworthy aspects of energy, vitality, and life. Betrayal, artistic or otherwise, is surely a form of moral disorder, inimical to both art and life, and therefore the legitimate object of a satirist's attack. But the speaker's charitable criticism, which is fictionally developed within the drama of the poem, expands the already established conflict between generosity of spirit in the Nisus-Euryalus episode and the lamented fact of unfulfilled expectations culminating later in the Marcellus-Oldham analogy.

The speaker's adept handling of his "critic's role" in the elegy has been universally admired as the epitome of poetic tact

11a. "Dryden's Panegyrics and Lyrics," in *John Dryden,* ed. Earl Miner (Athens: Ohio University Press, 1972), p. 140.

and control of tone. Clearly the characteristics of successful satire are not those necessarily required of all types of poetry, but prosodic and aural felicities, which this poem admirably demonstrates and the youthful Oldham has not accomplished, establish indisputably the speaker's "authority of tone," uniformly assumed in the great political satires of the 1680's. "Confidence," says Rachel Trickett, "is the keynote of [Dryden's satires], since it seems as if a mysterious division has been torn down between the reader's world and the poet's."[12] One of the chief delights of the Oldham elegy is the speaker's confident and assured manner in maintaining a gentle opposition between the idealizing tribute of a poet and the sober honesty of a practical critic. For Oldham there is praise, but for his poetry the praise is qualified. Expressions of grief and celebration of poetic achievement are combined with topical literary concerns. It is through a literary critique that the speaker establishes himself as critically aware and thus a competent judge of the truthfulness as well as the limitation of his imaginative ideal.

In this concern for both numbers and language, not only in the poetry of the dead Oldham but as demonstrated in the structural design of his own elegy, Dryden places a premium on the ordering powers of the poetic imagination. The question of poetic "numbers" in particular, of prosodic decorum in general, weighed heavily in Dryden's critical outlook as it did for other Augustan poets and influenced his whole theory and practice of translation and imitation. Through the power of the imagination the artist imitates those remote and idealized principles of order, harmony, and form; but he realizes this ideal realm, not only *through* the poem's conceptualizations but *in* the formal world of the poem's verbal structure.[13] This internal ordering constitutes art's "transforming," "redemptive," "restorative" (Battestin's terms) powers for the Augustan elegist, and his defense against the disorders felt in the actual experiencing of time and loss.

12.   Trickett, p. 57.

13.   My view here is reinforced in an interesting article by Robert D. Hume entitled "Dryden on Creation: 'Imagination' in the Later Criticism," *RES* (New Series) 21 (1970), 295 -314. Hume ostensibly continues the study of Dryden's concept of the imagination begun by John M. Aden ["Dryden and the Imagination: The First Phase," *PMLA,* 74 (1959), 28 -40] and finds that

Much has been written about the rhetorical felicities of the Oldham elegy, following T. S. Eliot's pronouncement that Dryden's unique poetic effect was "satisfying completeness of the statement."[14] Clearly the sententiousness and clarity of individual couplets balance nicely the more discursive movement of thought which results from effective grouping of couplets. A rich interplay of aural and metrical elements is also fully realized in the poem, as Van Doren detects with his finely attuned poetic ear.[15]

Thus the balance of competing rhetorical effects appropriately mirrors the familiar elegiac tensions between poetic ideal and poetic reality, between art and life, upon which the poem's final couplet focuses:

> Thy Brows with Ivy, and with Laurels bound;
> But Fate and gloomy Night encompass thee around. (24-25)

Poetic triumph, depicted in the traditional imagery of the bays, is played off against the unrelieved sense of mortality, symbolized by encircling and encompassing darkness and night, and images of poetic achievement are superimposed ironically on images acknowledging the victory of death. Moreover, circle imagery, alluding to the perfection and continuity of formal art, depicts the completion of a poet's life in the finality of death, just as the poem, itself permanent and immutable, depicts change, time, and mortality.[16]

The poem's structure can be described similarly as a harmonious tension of opposing forces. One force is centrifugal – generated by the allusive mode which constantly pushes the frame

---

instead of asserting "the autonomy of the fictive imagination" (Aden's phrase), Dryden, in his critical essays of the 1690's quite the contrary assumes a more orthodox neo-classical emphasis on "craft" and formal ordering of the creative imagination. "The evidence Aden finds for an incipiently Coleridgean [imagination] seems to me more than an intriguing part of the whole story. Dryden's occasional metaphors for creation are equally revealing, for craft and building are the terms generally chosen" (p. 313).

14. "John Dryden" (1922) in *Selected Essays* (London: Faber and Faber, 1932), p. 316.

15. *John Dryden: A Study of His Poetry* (New York: Holt, 1946), p. 66; also *Introduction to Poetry* (New York: Sloane, 1951), p. 97.

16. Dryden was of course notoriously opposed to shaped poems in the

of reference outward from the poem's center to include the widest possible meaning. Dryden and Oldham begin as fellow satirists in a friendly rivalry and end up not only as characters in Roman history but as epic figures who have achieved permanence as literary symbols preserved through an artifice which resists time and mortality. The other force is centripetal — generated by the tightly wrought rhetorical patterns which constantly exert control over the poem's inner design. The competing forces are finally complementary, providing in the compass of a single poem Dryden's version of an Augustan world "harmoniously confus'd." Still the experience of loss and time is real: even "the Muse herself that *Orpheus* bore" was powerless to change the course of nature, as Milton laments; and in describing Ransom's elegiac mode, Tate, we recall, carefully qualifies his definition: mastery of decay and death, he asserts, is always ironic because it is accomplished only through the celebrations of death itself.

Yet "To Mr. Oldham" reconciles the conflict between imaginative idealizations and the experience of time: psychologically, because it provides consolation through poetic ritual that links the living with the dead; aesthetically, because as poetic creations within the world of the poem both life and death are shaped by a viable, living tradition of elegiac expression into significant pattern. As a verbal construct the poem also provides assurance and consolation in its formal ordering of experience.

Dryden seems to affirm art's power to reconcile life and mortality, time and permanence, the ideal and the real,because in the elegy such contraries are not categorically opposed. Indeed, art is life made intelligible just as life formally rendered in the poem is made in the image of art. Dryden's speaker expresses confidence in art as an adequate compensation for time because he is under no illusions about its truths or limitations. He has faced the ironies implicit in the poetic transformation of life into art in the very poem which, as aesthetic object, affirms art's idealizing powers.

manner of George Herbert, for example. His mocking wit is no better demonstrated than in Flecknoe's advice to his poetic son:

    Leave writing Plays, and chuse for thy command
    Some peaceful Province in Acrostick Land. (205-206)

But we cannot help but notice that the coincidental first letter "O" in Oldham's name sustains the dominant image of these lines.

Commenting on Pope's whole literary career, Reuben Brower has said, for him "the imitation of life is also the imitation of literature."[17] This description is a fitting one for Dryden's own view of art as interpreter of human experience.

17. *Alexander Pope: The Poetry of Allusion* (Oxford: Clarendon Press, 1959), p. 361.

Chapter Three

A recent critic of Alexander Pope asserts that the mark of his Augustanism is "confidence in the power of the imagination to mediate between the ideal and the real."[1] To associate Pope's Augustanism with the role he assigns the imagination in life would seem on first consideration a perversely unorthodox reading of literary and intellectual history. Augustan poets are supposed to be realists, concerned with "man in his public aspects — general human nature — the permanent relations of human beings in society."[2] But the idea of the imagination as the poet's defense against time is not a uniquely romantic theory of art. In fact, the tensions inherent in just such a defense provide the dialectic of many of Pope's best poems. They dramatize this conflict between the idealizations of art and the facts of experience, while as verbal structures they reconcile the opposition in the permanence of form and the ideality of art.

The conflict between time and art accounts for the complexity of tone and style in many of Pope's best-known early poems. In *Windsor-Forest* (1713), for example, the view of contemporary England as an ideal society, like Milton's Eden of *Paradise Lost*, depends on the transforming power of the poetic imagination — the groves of Eden looking green in song. But this view is carefully qualified by references to the destructive violence connected with Windsor Forest, the various ruins of English history lying about, and the death and transfiguration of Lodona into a mythological figure. The pastoral note on which the poem ends warns the reader against taking the idealizing remarks about future British glory at face value. What the poet asserts and what time actually will bring are fundamentally irreconcilable, except

1. Thomas R. Edwards, Jr., *This Dark Estate: A Reading of Pope*, Perspectives in Criticism, No. 11 (Berkeley and Los Angeles, University of California Press, 1963), p. 12.
2. Maynard Mack, *The Augustans* (Englewood Cliffs, New Jersey: Prentice-Hall, 1950), p. 2

through the poem which embodies the ideal in the permanence of expression.

In the *Rape of the Lock* (1714), normally read as social satire, the dual themes of time and the imagination are fused in the certainty that the "quick" eyes of the sun-goddess Belinda "shall sett, as sett they must,"[3] and in the speaker's contrary assertion that the lock, a symbol of beauty no less than of vanity, will be inscribed permanently in the heavens as a comet. The fact of her beauty ironically emphasizes the pathos of mortality, the subject of Clarissa's speech in Canto V. But the ending of the poem would indicate that images of beauty (the lock), "out of nature," like Yeats's golden bird of Byzantium, will sing "Of what is past, or passing, or to come." The poem itself becomes an indestructible formulation of the defeat inflicted by time.

The *Epistle to Mr. Jervas* (1716) develops further the interplay between time and art, emphasizing the imagination's power over time and change, "build[ing] imaginary *Rome* a-new" (32). The illusion of life through art, the "living image in the Painter's breast" (42), is strongly asserted at the same time that it is qualified by the moral injunction typical of Augustan elegy:[4]

> Bid her [Elizabeth, Countess of Bridgewater] be all that chears or softens life,
> The tender sister, daughter, friend and wife;
> Bid her be all that makes mankind adore;
> Then view this marble, and be vain no more! (51-54)

But even here the mixture of regret and stern realism is expressed in the balanced phrasing and metrical symmetry that characterize couplet rhetoric. The speaker's ability to cope with reality by bringing poetic order out of his very acknowledgment of the chaos of time, loss, and death is art's way of redeeming time: it captures for posterity the poignancy of its evasions of reality. Both the illusion of artistic permanence and the realization of loss are brilliantly joined in the final couplet: "Alas! how little from the grave we claim? / Thou but preserv'st a Face and I a Name" (77-78).

3. *Poems of Alexander Pope*, ed. John Butt (New Haven: Yale University Press, 1963); all quotations of Pope's verse are from this one-volume edition of the Twickenham *Pope*.

4. See Paul Fussell, *The Rhetorical World of Augustan Humanism: Ethics and Imagery from Swift to Burke* (Oxford: Clarendon Press, 1965), p. 295.

Words asserting the permanence of art are balanced by words qualifying art's power over time, and thus create a tension of conflicting opposites — the mark of an Augustan poem. Pope's ability to sustain such a dual perspective is characteristic of the Augustan elegiac mode in general.

Pope's "Elegy to the Memory of an Unfortunate Lady" (1717) is his fullest exploration of the contrary claims of art and life. The poem can be read as emblematic of the opposition in Pope's mind between the idea of the imagination as an adequate defense against time and the recognition that the imagination is not an entirely satisfactory solution to the inescapable actualities of time. The story of the Unfortunate Lady is Pope's extended metaphor for the moral urgencies and attendant pathos of the experience of time, and the poem is his affirmation of life and beauty through the act of elegizing and the creation of order through poetic form. One of Milton's most perceptive modern readers has said that his great elegy, *Lycidas,* is a poem " 'about' poetry *and* 'about' human life — about the two in conjunction, man's vision of himself and the mirror of art in which he sees the vision."[5] Pope's "Elegy" explores this relationship between art and time, the ideal and the real, in eighteenth-century terms.

Although critics as far back as Joseph Warton have praised the "Elegy" for its powerful feelings and genuine sentiments, they appear to have based their reading almost exclusively on the question of Pope's relation with the Lady of the poem and on the moving coda (75 -82) in which he acknowledges his kinship with her and the fate of all mankind. More to the point is William K. Wimsatt's reading of the poem as one of Pope's "chief expressions in the pathetic and romantic mode."[6] By remarking Pope's range of styles, Wimsatt, like Reuben Brower in his description of the poem's "lyric sorrow and high declamation both laudatory and satirical,"[7] acknowledges the self-consciousness behind Pope's

5. Isabel G. MacCaffrey, "*Lycidas*: The Poet in a Landscape," in *The Lyric and Dramatic Milton,* ed. Joseph H. Summers (New York: Columbia University Press, 1965), p. 77.

6. *Selected Poetry and Prose of Alexander Pope,* ed. William K. Wimsatt, Jr. (New York: Rinehart, 1951), p. ix.

7. *Alexander Pope: The Poetry of Allusion* (Oxford: Clarendon Press, 1959), p. 65.

manipulation of rhetorical effects. Recently, Rachel Trickett has similarly responded to the "Elegy" by calling it "sentiment in the heightened rhetorical style."[8]

Pope's intentions are indicated at the outset: the melodramatic opening, the conscious allusion to Ben Jonson's elegy on Lady Jane Pawlet, and the reference to "acting" a "Lover's" or "*Roman's* part" (8) anticipate the theatrical treatment of emotion throughout. But the poem's fictional sorrow is finally viewed in the larger context of the speaker's experience of actual sorrow. Like the seriocomic effects of Pope's mock-heroic style in the *Rape of the Lock,* the mock-pathos of the "Elegy" constitutes a metaphor through which the poet deals with the serious issues raised by the facts of time, loss, and death. The final section of the "Elegy," like the last verse paragraph of *Lycidas,* shifts from a lyrical and narrative perspective to the personal reflections of the speaker-poet himself. Unlike *Eloisa to Abelard,* where the speaker tends to merge with the protagonists of the conflict, the speaker in the "Elegy" is detached so as to permit an objective commentary on events as they relate to his art and his own mortality.

The poem's structure is based on a series of contrasting views of death, as Thomas Edwards has shown.[9a] One view is contained in the plea, "Is there no bright reversion in the sky, / For those who greatly think, or bravely die? " (9-10). The opposite view is found in the speaker's acceptance of death and therefore of oblivion: "A heap of dust alone remains of thee; / 'Tis all thou art, and all the proud shall be! " (73-74). Between these extremes the speaker entertains several intermediate positions. One is the Christian notion of the soul moving out of the body at death "to its congenial place" (27). Still another possibility provides a satisfying retribution: the cruel guardian suffers the "sudden vengeance" of an "unlamented" death (37, 43). Finally, there is the conventional pastoral idea of the body reuniting with the timeless cycles of the natural world.

Pope sustains these opposed elegiac motifs in continuous tension. Every affirmation is matched with some kind of denial; a positive view of death as a kind of life means that a negative view of death as something final has been tested against the contrary

8. *The Honest Muse: A Study in Augustan Verse* (Oxford: Clarendon Press, 1967), p. 165.

8a. Edwards, pp. 22 -23.

claims. But these contraries are not merely static oppositions; they are felt as an organic interplay of self-qualifying propositions and feelings which the poet fully controls.

Such complexity is illustrated in the six-line section of the poem often noted for its "metaphysical wit." The main contrast here is between the current state of the Lady's soul — "Why bade ye else, ye Pow'rs! her soul aspire / Above the vulgar flight of low desire? " (11-12) — and the paralysis of spirit of the morally un-responsive:

> Most souls, 'tis true, but peep out once an age,
> Dull sullen pris'ners in the body's cage:
> Dim lights of life that burn a length of years,
> Useless, unseen, as lamps in sepulchres;
> Like Eastern Kings a lazy state they keep,
> And close confin'd to their own palace sleep. (17-22)

F. R. Leavis correctly views the change of imagery in the figure as effecting a shift in attitude toward the Lady's relatives.[9] But his point can be pressed further. The word "peep" undercuts the normally dignified, and often sacred, associations of the term "soul." The contrast between dignity and indignity carries over into the comparison of "souls" to prisoners, to dim lights in the "tomb" of the body, and to indolent monarchs. The comic idea of "peeping" is reinforced at the same time the line hints at the more serious implications of moral apathy — what Maynard Mack refers to as the death-in-life theme which the poem treats contemptuous-ly.[10] The meaning tends to expand from the notion of "souls" as "pris'ners" in the body to suggest darkness overcoming light, a frightening symbolism developed fully in the *Dunciad*. The word "age" (17) and the phrase "length of years" (19) establish the connection between the elegiac motif of time and the moral situation indicated by the passage. The certainty of time's effects on all men emphasizes by contrast the uncertain, fugitive nature of man's moral and spiritual responses.

9. *Revaluation: Tradition and Development in English* Poetry (London: Chatto & Windus, 1949), pp. 71-72.

10. " 'Wit and Poetry and Pope': Some Observations on His Imagery," in *Eighteenth-Century English Literature,* ed. James L. Clifford (New York: Oxford University Press, 1949), p. 23.

The passage contains some interesting qualifications of the ridicule directed at the Lady's relatives and at moral apathy in general. The souls are prisoners who can be released on good behavior or even escape their confines. The lamp is a light-giver, even though the light is obscured at present. Life symbols, then, are ironically present in the midst of physical and spiritual death. Pope's contemptuous view of human indifference at first would seem one-sided. But in the final analysis the symbols of time and death are qualified by these symbols of potential life.

This complex symbolism prepares the reader for the following section of the poem where the interplay between opposing motifs is expressed in a kind of pseudo-Renaissance diction, quasi-scientific and suggestive of cosmic matters in the style of Donne's *Anniversaries* or Dryden's ode to Anne Killigrew. Relying on his readers' sense of decorum, Pope blends "low" imagery of alchemy with "high" imagery derived from a Platonic-Christian theory of ecstasis. The Unfortunate Lady becomes the "purer spirits," and her oppressors become the "dregs" (25, 26). (Pope probably intended a pun on distilling,too.) The elegiac themes appear in line 23 in the parenthesis "(ere nature bade her die)," the tone of which lends a certain dignity to the act of dying and sustains the time and death imagery of the preceding "souls" passage. In addition, the formality of the parenthesis prepares the reader for the pastoral elegiac treatment of death later in the poem. The combination of conventional solemnity associated with Augustan personification and of references to the Lady's early death as an act of courtesy befitting her aristocratic background sustains the ironic contrast between the undignified circumstances of her death and the actual dignity of her dying (41-42). This series of contrasts also includes the theme of martyrdom which appeared early in the poem and set the stage for a miniature tragedy, a small-scale re-enactment of the prototypic Christian tragedy – of pride leading to the Fall and the subsequent introduction of time into human consciousness.[11]

11. Cf. Christopher Gillie, "Elegy to the Memory of an Unfortunate Lady," in *Interpretations: Essays on Twelve English Poems,* ed. John Wain (London: Routledge and Kegan Paul, 1955), pp. 77 -85. This highly existential reading of Pope's "Elegy" focuses on the interrelated motifs of ambition and compassion as part of a more inclusive theme: the value of human responsiveness.

The cosmic implication in the phrase "glorious fault of Angels and of Gods" (14) elevates the Lady's situation and underscores her dignity in contrast to her relatives' indignities, which are treated with scorn. The violence of such a contrast emphasizes the immense moral gulf between the Lady and her relatives and provides the conventional attack in elegy on persons or things hostile to the object of praise. Yet this paradoxical phrase, "glorious fault," with its exaggerated tone, gives a theatrical air to the whole passage:

> Ambition first sprung from your blest abodes;
> The glorious fault of Angels and of Gods:
> Thence to their Images on earth it flows,
> And in the breasts of Kings and Heroes glows! (13-16)

The inflated diction makes honorable the Lady's act of defiance, heightening while romanticizing it, but also making it vulnerable to elegiac irony. The claim for her transcendence cannot overcome the fact of her death. But the grandiose language and exaggerated emotion do not collapse the poem into sentimentality. These melodramatic shifts of tone characterize the violent alternations between heroic dignity and heightened pathos counterpointing the more somber elegiac motifs of loss and sadness.

These sudden shifts of tone within the "Elegy" are effective because of what Brower has called the "generous decorum" of the poem. Such modulation from the heroic mode or from the Petrarchan treatment of the dead Lady's former beauty (31-34) to the studied contempt for her guardian leads eventually to the pathos inherent in the conflict between symbols of life, permanence, or order and those of time, death, and confusion, to be found in the pastoral section (59 -69). The deepening despair over the special circumstances of the Lady's death receives appropriate accent in the rising crescendo of half- and full-line parallels so characteristic of Pope's rhetoric at times of high emotional tension:

> What can atone (oh ever-injur'd shade!)
> Thy fate unpity'd, and thy rites unpaid?
> No friend's complaint, no kind domestic tear
> Pleas'd thy pale ghost, or grac'd thy mournful bier;
> By foreign hands thy dying eyes were clos'd,
> By foreign hands thy decent limbs compos'd,
> By foreign hands thy humble grave adorn'd,
> By strangers honour'd, and by strangers mourn'd! (47-54)

The increased emotional intensity in depicting an ironic negation of value prepares the reader for an abrupt reversal of emotional thrust, as the absence of proper Christian burial rites becomes a positive distinction for the Lady:

> What tho' no weeping Loves thy ashes grace,
> Nor polish'd marble emulate thy face?
> What tho' no sacred earth allow thee room,
> Nor hallow'd dirge be mutter'd o'er thy tomb? (59-62)

A more extended version of this reversal effect occurs in the subsequent brilliant passage:

> Yet shall thy grave with rising flow'rs be drest,
> And the green turf lie lightly on thy breast:
> There shall the morn her earliest tears bestow;
> There the first roses of the year shall blow;
> While Angels with their silver wings o'ershade
> The ground, now sacred by thy reliques made. (63-68)

As Martin Price has shown, Pope, like Donne at the end of "The Canonization," creates two rival sets of images that bring about a reversal of value and of normal expectation within the elegiac context.[12] Through a fusion of Christian and pagan imagery, Pope develops the implications of one set of images associated with honors denied the Lady against another set of images viewing nature — of which the Lady is now a part — as ever-renewing and essentially benevolent. The tone of lines 59-62 betrays Pope's contempt for the "mockery of woe" (57). Like the statuary in Gray's famous abbey church, Pope's "weeping Loves," "polish'd marble," and "hallow'd dirge" seem ponderously grotesque, especially in the context of mock elevation provided by the two verbs "grace" and "emulate." By the time "mutter'd" occurs, the false emotion is exposed to the ironic gaze of the speaker. The reminders of death in the words "ashes" and "dirge" cancel further the possibility of consolation through ordinary mourning. Thus, satire is combined with elegiac emotion as it so often is in elegy.

12. *Swift's Rhetorical Art: A Study in Structure and Meaning* (New Haven: Yale University Press, 1953), pp. 40-41.

Reminders of death continue in lines 63-68, but receive heavy qualification by what Price calls the sense of "rising life" in the passage. Pope does not blunt the fact of the body's fertilization of the soil — thus the "rising flow'rs," "green turf," and blooming roses. Yet the actions of nature refer us back to a long line of elegiac laments, where nature conventionally responds to man's actions because he consciously relates to its operations and therefore denies any disparity between himself and nature. But the emphasis on mortality in lines 59 -62 is suddenly converted through the pastoral imagery into an affirmation of life in the ever-renewing organism of nature. The facts of death and loss remain with the speaker, but his attitude toward them has shifted. "Ashes" become "reliques"; "weeping Loves" are replaced by "Angels with their silver wings"; the literally profane "sacred earth" becomes ironically sacred "ground," an example of verbal irony in the reversal of normal associations of "earth" and "ground." This unexpected irony startles the reader into re-cognizing the emergence of dual elegiac motifs: life as death and death as life. The sense of ritual in the endless rotations of nature is suggested by such verbs as "drest," "bestow," and "blow." That the nature portrayed here is literary and stylized indicates both the poet's conscious manipulation of the elegiac attitudes generated by traditional pastoral imagery and his unembarrassed commitment to convention as metaphor.

The last eight lines of the poems (75-82) do not compromise the poem's literary tone, nor do they constitute a sudden, unprepared change from the basic fiction of stylized sorrow to the poet's "sincere" feelings and personal comment on time and mortality.[13] First of all,they are a kind of coda to the main poem, the final conclusion of a tentative conclusion the speaker has already reached in respect to the Lady's unfortunate story and its elegiac implications:

> So peaceful rests, without a stone, a name,
> What once had beauty, titles, wealth, and fame.
> How lov'd, how honour'd once, avails thee not,

13. Cf. Edwards, p. 23. This is where Edwards' otherwise accurate interpretation of Pope's "Elegy" goes wrong. He reads the conclusion as personally involving the writer Alexander Pope instead of a fictional poet-speaker objectively imagined.

To whom related, or by whom begot;
A heap of dust alone remains of thee;
'Tis all thou art, and all the proud shall be! (69-74)

This passage seems uncompromising in its appraisal of the fact of mortality; yet even it is consolatory, too, in the speaker's calm acceptance and epitaph-like tone. But in commenting on the Lady's situation, the last eight lines remind the reader of the function of epilogue in drama as commentary on preceding actions and themes of the work, in this case, on the resolution and conclusion of the fictional aspect of the elegy:

Poets themselves must fall, like those they sung;
Deaf the prais'd ear, and mute the tuneful tongue.
Ev'n he, whose soul now melts in mournful lays,
Shall shortly want the gen'rous tear he pays;
Then from his closing eyes thy form shall part,
And the last pang shall tear thee from his heart,
Life's idle business at one gasp be o'er,
The Muse forgot, and thou belov'd no more! (75-82)

By calling attention to Pope's poetic strategy, these lines also remind the reader of the differences between the world of the poem as a verbal artifact and the actual world in which he lives.

Throughout his career Pope was ambivalent about the importance of poetry and the ultimate value of artistic endeavor generally. He would identify, on the one hand, with Dennis' argument for poetry's "high seriousness," in fact, its virtual transcendent religious force in the *Essay on Criticism:*

Still green with Bays each *ancient* Altar stands,
Above the reach of *Sacrilegious* Hands. (181-182)

Or he would just as easily indulge in self-deprecation (partially ironic), labeling poets as silly in *Epistle II, i:*

We Poets are (upon a Poet's word)
Of all mankind, the creatures most absurd, (358-59)

and defining poetry as "by no means the universal concern of the world, but only the affair of idle men" (*Preface to Works,* 1717).[14]

14. See Emerson R. Marks, "Pope on Poetry and the Poet," *Criticism,* 12 (1970), 271 -80.

Here in the "Elegy" these lines are the poetic means of examining the claims of art's power over time and death. Art's validity and truthfulness to experience are paradoxically denied in the very medium that supposedly validates them. As a memorial to the "forgotten" Lady, the poem preserves her identity perpetually realized in the human capacity to respond to her plight. As a fixing of elegiac emotion into form, the poem represents the momentary triumph of artistic permanence and order over time and death.

A complex theory of the imagination is implicit in these lines of Pope, as it is in Milton's conclusion to *Lycidas*. Milton's speaker moves through a series of awarenesses reflected in the changing imagery and alternation of moods within the poem. The certainty with which he proclaims Christian hope and faith in the lines, "Weep no more, woeful Shepherds weep no more, / For *Lycidas* your sorrow is not dead," and his decision to cease lamenting the "sad occasion dear" have been reached only through his meditations on the injustice of early death and the universality of evil. Lycidas' ultimate achieving of a place among the saints is, naturally, a vision that is the special prerogative of the Christian poet. The "false surmise" of a pastoral paradise has been supplanted by a transfiguring vision tested and qualified by the facts of experience and understood only as symbolic representation of ultimate reality, life at the remove of art. This recognition accounts for the change in tone and perspective in the final eight lines of *Lycidas*. The words "Thus sang the uncouth swain" underscores the fact that what has transpired in the "Doric Lay" is artistic vision, but a vision nonetheless relevant in the actual world of experience. As an act of the imagination, it is the poet's way of accounting for his idealizations and acknowledging their value as such, even as he recognizes the limitations of art. The shift to third person and the broadening of the visual perspective impersonalize, objectify, and therefore generalize the speaker's insight for all men. What was private and subjective has become public and representative.

Pope's poem ends with a comparable insight. The narrative is the source of elegiac feeling, and the poet's self-conscious use of conventional devices of style, the means by which he heightens and exaggerates emotion: the elegiac motifs are artificially stimulated and so elaborately "literary" that they achieve the effect of pastoral elegy. Contrary to Ralph Cohen's contention that "Pope's

ceremonial and allusive language — 'prais'd ear' and 'tuneful tongue' and melting lays — brings to the fore the incapacity of
ceremony to make the momentary permanent," the "Elegy" in its
commitment to art and artifice belies the "statements" made in
these final lines about time and mutability.[14a] What seems contradictory is actually Pope's version of the doctrine that "the truest
poetry is the most feigning."

The relationship of the imagination and art to reality — how
poetry is "true" and how it is "feigning" — is a dominant theme in
Pope's work. In his Horatian poems, of course, Pope was acutely
conscious of the power of satire to effect moral reform as well as
to provide political opposition to the Walpole ministry. The
Epilogue to the Satires, especially *Dialogue II,* is eloquent testimony to his almost desperate faith in the morality of art and the
ethical responsibility of the poetic voice (O sacred Weapon! left
for Truth's defence" 212). But in a different vein Pope also
concedes life-giving powers to the poet's creative imagination as
late as 1737, in his partial translation of the ninth Ode of Horace,
Book Four:

> Sages and Chiefs long since had birth
> > E're Caesar was, or Newton nam'd,
> These rais'd new Empires o'er the Earth,
> > And Those new Heav'ns and Systems fram'd;
>
> Vain was the chief's and sage's pride
> > They had no Poet and they dyd!
> In vain they schem'd, in vain they bled
> > They had no Poet and are dead!(9-16)

Here the poet is credited with immortalizing the otherwise transient existences of the famous and learned.

But in the final eight lines of the "Elegy," Pope treats the
theme as Milton does in the conclusion to *Lycidas.* Although
setting, imagery, and protagonists differ, the poetic strategy is
similar.[15] Milton alters the perspective of *Lycidas* by means of

---

14a. Ralph Cohen, "The Augustan Mode in English Poetry," *ECS,* 1
(1967), 20.

15. Trickett distinguishes the pastoral elegy from Augustan elegy this
way: "Beginning with lamentation and ending with consolation, it brought
life and death into a new relationship and resolved the poet's grief by

syntactical dislocations of time, changes in tone and voice, and a redefinition of pastoral. The fictional day comprising the shepherd's timeless meditation becomes an actual day of responsible labors in the field. This shift provides the disengagement that assures the poem's "anonymity," as John Crowe Ransom calls it, an impersonal rendering of a personal experience. In the "Elegy" Pope shifts from a narrative mode to generalized speculation about the implications of that narrative. Pope's speaker steps outside the story and comments on his role in fashioning it. Words like "sung," "tuneful tongue," "melts," and "mournful lays" refer to the elegizing in the poem. The references to the Lady's "form" and her "prais'd ear" suggest that she owes both her life and death to the poet's creative imagination, the "Muse" of line 82. But the elegiac paradox is sustained to the very end, where poet and his "idle business" of life – writing poetry — seem subject irrevocably to the operations of time. Milton's strategy at the end of *Lycidas* clearly indicates his final acknowledgment that the vision of a transcendent Lycidas is symbolic, not to be enacted in the actual world of the shepherd. For Pope's speaker, response to time and death has brought a similar recognition of the limits of art.[16] The poetic act, like all such imaginative projections, dehumanizes feeling into the permanence of form. But the poet's detachment – his "negative capability," in Keats's phrase — proves the ultimate triumph of art over time. For art, even when it expresses its own

an apotheosis. But this not the elegiac mood of Augustan verse" (p. 23). This is only partly true for *Lycidas* and does not account for the shifted perspective in the final eight lines.

16. Cf. Howard D. Weinbrot, "Pope's 'Elegy to the Memory of an Unfortunate Lady,' " *MLQ*, 32 (1971), 255 -67. Although acknowledging Pope's "contemporary practice" around the time of 1717, Weinbrot strenuously objects to reading the "Elegy" in terms of a conflict between "permanent art" and "transient nature," or as utilizing his "familiar device of proclaiming the subject's life in art." I agree with Weinbrot's insistence on separating the "distraught poet-narrator" from the biographical Pope "characteristically moral, Christian, and anti-pagan." But he errs, I think, in drawing an easy analogy between the art-nature, moral, and religious themes, especially in his inference that the poem's conclusion rejects "the convention of the permanence of art" (p. 267). The poem surely cannot self-destruct; it stands as continual testimony to Pope's acting through poetry even upon a view that qualifies the claim to permanent art.

limitations, is his instrument of understanding and acceptance of the human condition. An awareness of art's truth as well as its limitations, Pope seems to say, provides the only possible consolation for time, loss, and death. But it is the supreme consolation of understanding one's basic humanity.

Chapter Four

In his review of the Oxford Edition of Matthew Prior's literary works, Maynard Mack calls "An Epitaph" (1718) "one of the fine poems... of the eighteenth or any other century." Whatever the standard of evaluation, this is an impressive claim for what is surely a minor Augustan poet's minor poem, indeed one rather begrudgingly described by Samuel Johnson as "among the best of Prior's lighter pieces." But one explanation for Mack's praise is the contemporaneity of the poem's theme and sentiments: an age, he suggests, which finds "its own image in Eliot's 'Hollow Men' and gives rise to existentialist agonies at the absurdity yet necessity of commitment"[1] would immediately recognize the ironic praise and sorrow expressed for this thoroughly undistinguished, listless, sterile couple — an eighteenth-century, pre-urban version of the computerized, dehumanized, organizational stereotype so memorably caricatured in W. H. Auden's "Unknown Citizen."

Although strikingly modern in theme, if not in its ironic method, Prior's mock elegy is very much a poem of its age. The irony in "An Epitaph" derives partly from the style itself — the tone, rhetorical devices, and versification effects — and partly from conventions and intellectual traditions informing the poem from the outside.

One tradition clearly behind the satire is the stoic ideal of self-sufficient virtue and the related theme of retirement. Prior pictures Jack and Joan of the poem as middle-class travesties of this stoic ideal. They, Prior seems to say, represent the realities of this ethic.

Anti-stoical bias was strong in eighteenth-century England, especially among the Augustan humanists.[2] Pope's "Stoic's pride," Fielding's exposure of Parson Adams, and Johnson's philosopher

---

1. "Matthew Prior: *Et Multa Prior Arte,*" review of Prior's Works, in *Sew R,* 68 (1960), 173, 174.

2. See Henry W. Sams, "Anti-stoicism in seventeenth and early eighteenth-century England," *SP,* 41 (1944), 65 -78.

in Chapter 18 of *Rasselas* are familiar examples of this constant ridicule. Monroe K. Spears, in a thorough examination of Prior's ethical thought, connects his poetry in general, and "An Epitaph" in particular, with the wide gap between stoic doctrine and belief and the stresses of real life. "Passions are the stuff of human life," Spears claims for Prior, "and to excise them is to throw off humanity."[3]

This is not to say that Prior is a Hobbesian working in the libertine tradition of a Rochester to justify the morality of passions on the basis of their naturalness. Yet portions of his respected "Jinny the Just" (1708) do indicate the importance in life of feeling and emotion, and Prior's awareness of the complexity of human motivation:

> From some real Care but more fancied vexation
> From a life party: colour'd half reason half passion
> Here lyes after all the best Wench in the Nation.[4] (7-9)

The speaker goes on to commend Jinny's singleness of purpose:

> And Her will with her duty so equally stood
> That Seldom oppos'd she was commonly good
> And did pretty well, doing just what She wou'd. (52-54)

Her commitment to life and the world and her essential humanity are summarized in the following triplet:

> While she read and accounted and pay'd and abated
> Eat and drank, play'd and work't, laught and cry'd, lov'd and hated
> An answer'd the End of her being created. (85-87)

In "An Epitaph," by contrast, Prior presents, in a deadpan tone, the couple's laconic response to the world around them:

> And having bury'd Children Four,
> Wou'd not take Pains to try for more.

***

3. "Some Ethical Aspects of Matthew Prior's Poetry," *SP,* 45(1948), 608.

4. *The Literary Works of Matthew Prior,* ed. H. Bunker Wright and Monroe K. Spears, 2 vols. (Oxford: Clarendon Press, 1959); all quotations of Prior's verse are from this edition.

Each Virtue kept it's proper Bound,
Nor Trespass'd on the other's Ground.

***

They gave the Poor the Remnant-meat,
Just when it grew not fit to eat.

***

They paid the Church and Parish-Rate;
And took, but read not the Receit:
For which They claim'd Their *Sunday's* Due,
Of slumb'ring in an upper Pew.

***

No Man's Defects sought They to know;
So never made Themselves a Foe.

***

When Bells were Rung, and Bonfires made;
If ask'd, They ne'er deny'd their Aid.

(13-14, 19-20, 31-32, 33-36, 37-38, 51-52)

Closely allied with the stoical ideal is the retirement myth, equally important to the context of "An Epitaph" by virtue of its burlesque embodiment in the persons of Jack and Joan. Images and attitudes of retirement, which the Augustans inherited from their Roman predecessors and seventeenth-century English imitators, are grotesquely distorted in the life and times of this infamous couple.

As activist-diplomat and man of world affairs, Prior could not be expected to urge self-cultivation and contemplation as a way of life. But he appears to acknowledge this concept of man as a possible alternative, at least as a literary ideal by which to measure the present circumstance. The epigraph to "An Epitaph" from Seneca's second chorus in *Thyestes* compels the reader to view Prior's lament in the context and idiom of retirement literature:

Stet quicunque volet potens
Aulae culmine lubrico, & C.

This epigraph alone seems little more than the clichéd warning of dangers attending the pride and power of court life, merely a one-dimensional ironic reference to the various anti-stoical sentiments informing the poem. But to ignore the whole context of such an allusive phrase in Prior, or in any other Augustan poet, is to risk missing the metaphoric force of a literary and historical past on the present situation. A fuller reading of the chorus goes like this:

> Let him stand who will, in pride of power, on empire's
> slippery height; let me be filled with sweet repose;
> in humble station fixed, let me enjoy untroubled ease,
> and to my fellow citizens unknown, let my life's
> stream flow in silence. So when my days have
> passed noiselessly, lowly may I lie and full of years.
> On him does death lie heavily, who, but too well known
> to all, dies to himself unknown.[5]

This chorus clearly provides for Prior, I think, the focus of values he sees lacking, not so much in the active life as such, but in the unexamined and unaware existence of these eighteenth-century counterparts of the modern absurd. The resonances and assumptions behind this passage are legion, as Mack has also convincingly shown, providing both theme and poetic convention for writers as diverse as Marvell, Cowley, Dryden, Pope, to mention only a few prominent examples.[6] Recollection of the positive force of these models, say, in Pope's "On Solitude," *Windsor-Forest, Moral Essay I,* or the Horatian poems is to recognize the positive standards implicit in "An Epitaph." Prior exposes the corruption of indifference which infects outer and inner life-styles, actions and moral attitudes, by recreating for himself, through theme and structure, both ethical and aesthetic realities associated with the retirement myth as literary ideal.

For the Augustans, aesthetic performance was inseparable from ethical prescription, and their interdependence is eloquently expressed in a famous passage from Pope's *Epistle II, ii,* published nineteen years after Prior's poem:

---

5. Quoted from "Review of Prior's Works," p. 174.

6. *The Garden and the City: Retirement and Politics in the Later Poetry of Pope 1731-1743* (Toronto: University of Toronto Press, 1969), especially **pp.** 79 -115.

To Rules of Poetry no more confin'd,
I learn to smooth and harmonize my Mind,
Teach ev'ry Thought within its bounds to roll,
And keep the equal Measure of the Soul.(202-205)

This ironic dismissal of poetry for the higher art of living is paradoxically couched in the language and metaphor of literary criticism — "smooth," "harmonize," "equal Measure." Such a passage equates mastery over mind with the power to control and harmonize the human faculties. The creation of art becomes the creation of selfhood. It is this happy relationship between art and life, creative principle and the moral obligation, which Prior satirically establishes in its breach. The controlled style ("Thought within its bounds"), harmonious adjustment of diction with tone — in short, the poem's morality of satirical art is heightened through contrast with the moral chaos of bad living in the poem. "An Epitaph" exhibits the fusion of creative and controlling energies sadly missing in the desultory existence of Jack and Joan.

Prior's combined tones of comic amusement and satiric condemnation are sustained by a style of expression which resembles Gay, or even Swift in his lighter moments. It is a style perfectly demonstrating the economy of diction, play of wit, and finesse of allusion and parody we expect not only in Augustan lapidary verse, but in the best neo-classical satire:

INTERR'D beneath this Marble Stone,
Lie Saunt'ring JACK,and Idle JOAN.
While rolling Threescore Years and One
Did round this Globe their Courses run.

***

Without Love, Hatred, Joy, or Fear,
They led — a kind of — as it were:
Nor Wish'd, nor Car'd, nor Laugh'd, nor Cry'd:
And so They liv'd; and so They dy'd.(1-4, 59-62)

These opening lines (1-4), which parody ancient inscriptions on Latin and Greek tombstones, are nicely balanced by the closing verse (59-62), mocking conventional elegiac sentiments. It is a rhetoric marked by insistent alliteration and syntactical repetition, as well as by the heavy use of parallelism and antithesis characteristic of couplet rhetoric. His use of octosyllabics presents to the reader a peculiar variation of the "sense of continually fulfilled expectation," which Northrop Frye notes in the heroic couplet of Pope.[7] Instead of Pope's rich ambiguities, startling juxtapositions, or sudden modulation of tones, Prior creates in his metrical patterns an "expectation" of regularity and predictable economy of language appropriate to the matter-of-fact character of the couple's existence. The easy swing of phrase, fluid versification, and to-and-from movements within a line and between verses imitate the hesitant, nonchalant life of Jack and Joan.

Key verbs (emphasized by alliteration) and adjectives depict the couple's circumstances in diction echoing elegiac feeling common to seventeenth-century meditations on time and mortality. The world that Prior creates moves ominously through time, and in this purposeless motion without force and in the negation of life and human emotion, Jack and Joan become an undifferentiated part of the inexorable passing of time. In fact, the diction of passivity and stasis ("Lie," "Interr'd," "Marble," etc.), as well as the strong feeling of past tense, merely accentuates by contrast both process and time, and therefore the deaths underscored by the presence of the tombstone and the elegiac action itself.

This elegiac irony, punctuated by the interplay of internal and end rhymes and the sharply expressed antitheses, contributes to the racy comic tone sustained throughout the elegy. The peculiar ambling rhythms of the following couplet reveal how funny the seemingly straightforward and simple can be:

> They Walk'd and Eat, good Folks: What then?
> Why then They Walk'd and Eat again. (8-10)

The repetition of "Walk'd and Eat," the two "Theys" and "thens" arranged, as they are rhetorically, into question-answer sequence arouse the desire for some sort of narrative resolution. Instead, this repetition device only accentuates the tone of contempt, and also mitigates slightly the fact of this dreary, repetitive life-style by a touch of playfulness.

7. "Towards Defining an Age of Sensibility," in *Eighteenth-Century English Literature: Modern Essays in Criticism,* ed. James L. Clifford (New York: Oxford University Press, 1959), p. 313.

Comic elegiac tone is maintained by the constant interplay between manner and matter, style and theme. One of Prior's favorite devices, for example, is to place antithesis in a position to receive major stress in the second half of a line. This juxtaposition of opposites has the poetic effect of reinforcing the couple's moral aimlessness and human failure:

> If Human things went Ill or Well;
> If changing Empires rose or fell. (5-6)

Or in a variation on this pattern, the antithesis alternates from the first half of the couplet's initial verse to the second half position in the first line of the couplet:

> Nor Tear, nor Smile did they imploy
> At News of Public Grief,or Joy.

> ***

> Nor Fame, nor Censure They regarded:
> They neither Punish'd, nor Rewarded. (49-50, 21-22)

In both couplets rhythmic expectations, contrasting diction, and parallel phrasing of opposed meanings reinforce the ambulatory motions and moral ambivalence of Jack and Joan.

Another example of sound and sense interplay occurs when Prior arranges phrases in parallel position to alternate in rapid succession so as to spill over in exuberant feminine rhyming:

> They neither Added, nor Confounded:
> They neither Wanted, nor Abounded. (45-46)

A modification of this effect takes place when half-lines qualify one another,resulting in mild irony:

> Their Beer was strong; Their Wine was *Port*;
> Their Meat was large; Their Grace was short. (29-30)

In the first two half-lines the drink and food are identified with positive modifiers like "strong" and "large," whereas by contrast "Wine" and "Grace" are depreciated by "Short" and *"Port"* (according to the Oxford note a cheap and popular wine imported at low rates from Portugal). By this peculiar location of phrases,

Prior throws wine tastes and prayer into unholy alliance. It is no surprise that, as with all aspects of Jack and Joan's lives, materialistic considerations outweigh any ethical or serious spiritual obligation. Indeed, economic needs and desires triumph over Christmas, and clearing accounts replaces the traditional expressions of generosity and Christian charity:

> Each *Christmas* They Accompts did clear;
> And wound their Bottom round the Year. (47-48)

Instead of elegance and beauty Prior utilizes a spare diction and generally deliberate, almost mechanical, style of presentation to express these prosaic lives. This practice might seem to open the poem to the charge of simplistic realism or the so-called imitative fallacy, risking overall unity and coherence for the sake of "local expressiveness."[8] As readers of modern poems like Pound's *Cantos* and Eliot's *The Waste Land,* we can distinguish between the illusion of chaos and coherent rhetorical design and the identifiable symbolic patterns which create this illusion of disorder. A similar transformation is felt in "An Epitaph." Prior does not write a boring poem about dull, pedestrian individuals in order to exemplify Augustan demands for verisimilitude. Rather, his localized rhetorical devices provide a style congruent with characterization, narrative action, and satirical intention without slavish imitation.

Prior's art and artifice have been patronized by the poet William Cowper as "easy jingle." This judgment is both defensible and misleading, depending on whether we view this "jingling" as an end in itself or as functional to the comic and satiric intentions. To judge by example of Prior's mock-elegy, the "jingle" is precisely the stylistic feature which rescues the poem from the mediocrity of literalism or realism. "An Epitaph" exhibits Dryden's point about octosyllabics in his *Progress of Satire.* Much as Johnson's understandable but wrongheaded critique of *Lycidas* focuses on

8. For a mostly hostile account of Pope's experiments in "local expressiveness," see Irvin Ehrenpreis, "The Style of Sound: The Literary Value of Pope's Versification," in *The Augustan Milieu: Essays presented to Louis A. Landa,* eds. Henry Knight Miller, Eric Rothstein, and G. S. Rousseau (New York: Oxford University Press, 1970), pp. 232-246.

inescapable aesthetic problems, Dryden's strong disapproval of the short couplet highlights the effect Prior so successfully exploits. Undignified, perhaps, and appropriate only to light ridicule or cavalier amusement, the style of "An Epitaph" keeps the satire kindly and lighthearted in its serious sort of way. This comic perspective is possible only because of the humorous irony sustained in the jostle and bounce of the verse. Detachment, the ability to take a wry perspective on the everyday world, is the condition of art, and is ultimately connected with the ability of the imagination to transform dull activities and moral failures into ideal aesthetic and moral orders — where decorum, wit, and irony indicate a sense of self, of civility and charity eternally at war with pettiness, pride, tastelessness, and indifference.

Prior once wrote (half-jokingly) in "For His Own Epitaph": "we flatter our Selves, and teach Marble to lye." This assertion is instructive since it, like all such revelations, touches on the relationship between imagination and reality, art and life. But as with such negative statements about art's truthfulness and its adequacy as a defense against time, it cannot escape the irony of existing as an expression of art itself. This seeming dismissal of art is not in fact Prior's final say on the sincerity of elegiac sentiments or the validity of art. For in the same poem a contrary but poignant assertion creates the tension of opposites characteristic of the Augustan elegiac mode:

> This Verse little polish'd thô mighty sincere
> > Sets neither his Titles nor Merit to view,
> It says that his Relicks collected lye here,
> > And no Mortal yet knows too if this may be true. (21 -24)

Skeptical, yes, but this stanza insists that man's worldly pursuits ("Titles," "Merit") have also a reality and validity in their own right and that the practice of this "mighty sincere" art can save thought and feeling (a poet's "Relicks") from the ravages of time. The elegist, therefore, shapes in his imagination and art a moral world in fictional imitation of the larger order of Nature, a moral order unknown to the likes of Jack and Joan.

By comically treating familiar elegiac themes and conventions, Prior, in "An Epitaph," reminds man of the gulf between the possible and the actual in human life and manner as well, if only by establishing through his comic rendition a contrast between serious Augustan elegizing and its debasement as memorial to this contemptible couple. Such a comic transformation constitutes the nature of art's permanence and power over time. Prior's "An Epitaph" makes boredom and mediocrity memorable through comical satire, and in its function as "friend to man," in Keats's phrase, affirms the capacity of art to preserve life and meaning from the destructiveness of time and mortality.

Chapter Five

Both creative and critical writing in the English Augustan Age were often shaped by the requirements and expectations of genre. Because their minds were accustomed to hierarchical determinations, the literary men of the age easily categorized and classified works of literature by distinct types and modes, distinguishing between the language and style of, say, epic and pastoral or comedy and satire. This predetermination of forms of expression resulted in the observance of literary decorum, and all the restrictions and methodology such a doctrine entails. Even sympathetic readers often decry the artificiality and literariness of Augustan literature.

But the examples of Fielding, Pope, and Swift, to mention only three, would suggest that these constraints of genre actually release creative energy and poetic genius. Again and again these writers purposely exploit the formal expectations of genre to create complex literary effects. Fielding describes *Tom Jones* as a "comic epic poem in prose," and utilizes devices and techniques of classical epic in the book for comic purposes. Pope's most famous exercise in the mock-epic, addressed to Mrs. Arabella Fermor, carries the hedging subtitle "An Heroi-Comical Poem," and treats a trivial episode as though it were heroic action. Swift unabashedly calls his elegy to Marlborough "Satirical Elegy on a Late Famous General," mocking the conventions and sentiments of formal elegy.

This mixing of techniques and styles is especially characteristic of Augustan elegiac and satirical modes of expression. Like Dryden's proverbial "Great Wits" and "Madness," elegy and satire are just as closely "ally'd." The impulse to praise and lament or blame often occurs in the same literary work. As Paul Fussell has nicely phrased it, "To write satire is implicitly to undertake elegiac action, for all satire assumes some identifiable paradigm of virtue which folly has willingly let die."[1] Or viewed from the elegist's

---

1. *The Rhetorical World of Augustan Humanism: Ethics and Imagery from Swift to Burke* (Oxford: Clarendon Press, 1959), p. 283.

perspective, "the celebration of virtue must be an elegy,"[2] as Thomas Edwards points out. While satire essentially condemns, it does so against positive standards, norms, or affirmations, and these idealizations are implicitly the subject of elegy. Thus Dryden's *Absalom and Achitophel* includes idealized portraits of Charles's loyalists and even of a mythical monarch symbolizing political stability, order, and sacramental human loyalties, while Milton's *Lycidas* includes a satirical attack on corrupt clergy.

Swift's controversial "Verses on the Death of Dr. Swift" (1731) contains just such a mixture of sentiment and styles. Ostensibly it is elegy, but treatment of the poem always raises the issue of its satirical intention and ironical method, especially as relates to the function of the puzzling eulogy (307-384) spoken by "One quite indiff'rent in the Cause " (305).[3] But this predictable approach creates little agreement as to the poem's meaning. John Middleton Murry, for instance, calls the ending "unqualified eulogy" in "flat contradiction to the first part,"[4] whereas Barry Slepian reads the end as pure irony, the logical conclusion of Swift's thesis "that all mankind is egotistical, selfish, and proud."[5] Marshall Waingrow argues a still more complex case, acknowledging that Swift's own vanity is emphatically demonstrated but that the whole thrust of the poem "shows that *his* vanity is knowledgeable, that it doesn't disguise his kinship with other men, and that upon such knowledge virtue may be built."[6] More recently, John Irwin Fischer, in what amounts to a long footnote to Waingrow's argument, also minimizes the satire. He views the poem as "a personal, deeply searching and . . . very traditional consideration by Swift of the implications of his own death,"[7] and explains the

2. *This Dark Estate: A Reading of Pope,* Perspectives in Criticism, No. 11 (Berkeley and Los Angeles: University of California Press, 1963), p. 94.

3. *The Poems of Jonathan Swift,* ed. Harold Williams, 3 vols. (2nd ed.; Oxford: Clarendon Press, 1958). All quotations of Swift's poetry are from this edition.

4. *Jonathan Swift: A Critical Biography* (London: Cape, 1954), p. 458.

5. "The Ironic Intention of Swift's Verses on his own Death," *RES,* 14 (1963), 256.

6. " 'Verses on the Death of Dr. Swift,' " *SEL,* 5 (1965), 513.

7. "How to Die: 'Verses on the Death of Dr. Swift,' " *RES* (New Series) 21 (1970), 424.

poem's complexity by means of seventeenth-century meditative materials and traditional Christian approaches to death familiar to eighteenth-century readers in Scripture, the Prayer Book, and homiletics.

A better approach, it seems to me, is to analyze the interplay in Swift's "Verses" between the satirical effects and the elegiac sentiments and design, especially as related to the familiar tensions inherent in the idea of the imagination as a defense against time and mortality, and to the more fundamental opposition between art and time at the heart of the Augustan elegiac mode.

Swift continually dramatizes these conflicting elegiac motifs, often couching them in witty but scathing indictments of human indifference, folly, and smug self-interest:

Why do we grieve that Friends should dye?
No Loss more easy to supply. (243-44)

Here the pathos associated with death is counteracted by a sense of relief resulting from abrogation of moral responsibility, in this case, a gross perversion of the traditional consolation felt in the ritual celebration of death — the act of elegizing itself. A more "heart-less" reaction to Swift's death is accomplished through the imagined ladies's card game gossip, in which conventional pathos and sentiment are degraded by the empty elegiac cliché, which exposes moral apathy and callous indifference to the human predicament:

"His Time was come, he ran his Race;
We hope he's in a better Place." (241-42)

Such hope is hardly fervent, and the jaunty, sleazy tone conflicts with the compensating affirmations of life and permanence accomplished by the formal ordering of emotion through convention alive with value.

This flippant quality gives way to seriousness, and the oppressive sense of loss extends from poet to his works and reputation:

One Year is past; a different Scene;
No further mention of the Dean;
Who now, alas, no more is mist,
Than if he never did exist. (245-248)

Swift's unsentimental view of the actualities of time and mortality expressed in these lines excludes self-pity or a self-indulgent rupture of tone by the detached bitterness felt in the commonplace diction and deadpan style.

The poet intensifies the grim reality of changing tastes and sensibilities, this time speaking in a cavalier way through the voice of the publisher Lintot about presumptuous faith in imaginative idealizations and the permanence of art:

> "To fancy they cou'd live a Year!
> I find you're but a Stranger here.
> The Dean was famous in his Time;
> He had a Kind of Knack at Rhyme:
> His way of Writing now is past;
> The Town hath got a better Taste." (261-66)

These lines accurately express with their characteristically dry, understated irony the compelling awareness and heightened sensitivity of Swift to loss. They comprise his sarcastic challenge to the ancient aphorism "life is short but art is long."

Locating the positive moral standards which lie behind his satire has been the unending despair of Swift's readers from the eighteenth century on, and his positive view of art's power over time is also never openly stated. In fact, the usual emphasis in Swift criticism is on his alleged "negativism" toward most things. Herbert Davis's uncompromising pronouncement that Swift was the "most extreme example . . . in England of reaction against the heroic or romantic view of the poet's function and art"[8] gives some pause, as does the whole succeeding body of critical opinion which declares Swift anti-art, anti-poetic, anti-romantic, "anti" about everything. True, there are numerous examples both in his well-known and not so familiar poems, as well as in parts of *A Tale of a Tub,* which ridicule anything close to "enthusiasm," "visionary," "inspiration," "fancy." Swift at times clearly indicates an almost innate fear of "poetick Fire" and even of language itself as a distortion of reality. The extent of these claims of Swift's negative attitude toward art can be understood by the words of a recent critic who asserts that Swift has lost "confidence in the capacity of serious poetic forms – of poetic language – to express all that he needs to express." "It is as though Swift," in contrast to Pope, Johnston continues, "were serving notice on all readers of poetry, warning them that he will systematically

---

8. Swift's View of Poetry," in *Jonathan Swift: Essays on his Satire and Other Studies* (New York: Oxford University Press, 1964), p. 163.

demolish the standards of poetic language that they normally rely on."[9]

Yet for all of his debunking of poetry and art — even "Verses" contains a tongue-in-cheek reference to the inevitable "Grub-Street Wits" who will flood the town with elegies "To *curse* the *Dean,* or *bless* the *Drapier"* — Swift indirectly affirms the ideal of art as a defense against time, ironically transforming the fact of death through the creation of poetic order and form. Normally, death for a poet is the most significant event in his life since it can give him immortality and everlasting fame; but Swift engineers his immortality through a fictional account of his own death. Unlike the Yeats of W. H. Auden's famous tribute, it is Swift's "death" which is recorded by art, and it is through this "death" that Swift's life and art are preserved.[10] Ironically, then, the imaginative "death" affirms the power of art to salvage reality from time.

The poem develops these oppositions between art and life in a number of ways, combining conventions of elegy with those of satire. The second part of "Verses" (73-298), for example, can be viewed as an ironic variation of the conventional procession of mourners and ritualistic strewing of the bier with flowers as in pastoral elegy. Instead of meaningful ritual, which links the living with the dead, Swift substitutes the mindless and heartless verbal reactions of "special Friends," aristocratic ladies, and "those I love" for a satirical strike at human selfishness.

These same oppositions are implicit in the broader framework of the poem. Elegy traditionally begins on a note of loss and regret and ends on a note of consolation and acceptance of the fact of death. The speaker's experiences with time and change bring him into some new understanding that can lead to acceptance of actuality. This changed relationship between

9. Oswald Johnston, "Swift and the Common Reader," in *In Defense of Reading: A Reader's Approach to Literary Criticism,* ed. Reuben A. Brower and Richard Poirier (New York: E. P. Dutton), pp. 179, 181. Swift wrote to Charles Wogan in 1732, describing himself as a "man of rhymes" undeserving of the exalted "Muses Lyre." See *Correspondence of Jonathan Swift,* ed. Harold Williams (Oxford: Clarendon Press, 1965), IV, p. 52. Hereafter cited as *Correspondence.*

10. Auden's lines go as follows: "By mourning tongues/ The death of the poet was kept from his poems."

speaker and event accounts for the sequence of awareness depicted in the three sections of the poem. Swift's "Swift" imagines the responses to his own death in order to demonstrate the elegist's defense against time. Recognition of his fictive representation of self in the elegy, rather than simplifying and dehumanizing the historical Jonathan Swift contemplating mortality, sharpens and intensifies his view of life and death and contributes to our fuller understanding of the poem's elegiac design.

Like his fellow satirist Pope, Swift is often chided for a strong strain of self-justification in his role as defender of public morality, and "Verses" contains its share of such insistent, if expected, literary apologias:

> "Fair LIBERTY was all his Cry;
> For her he stood prepar'd to die."

***

> "Yet, Malice never was his Aim;
> He lash'd the Vice but spar'd the Name."

***

> "His Satyr points at no Defect,
> But what all Mortals may correct." (347-48; 459-60; 463-64)

Even if these lines are ironic praise, this would not totally undercut the force and persuasiveness carried by the emphatic tone and asserted truthfulness of the language. The satirist often creates imagined selves who function as sharp dramatizations of good and evil, virtue and vice, country and court — or Houyhnhnm and Yahoo. The actual and personal are always suppressed in favor of these fictional, if simplified, oppositions.

The pursuit of truth is, of course, the satirist's motivating ethos, and no diversion, not even literary fame itself, will deter him from this goal. Pope's Horatian poems and the *Epistle to Dr. Arbuthnot* strenuously assert, at key points in the poems, the independence and moral integrity of the poet. The strategy often calls for the illusion of shattering the consciously manipulated satiric mask in order to condemn vice in frank, sincere, and passionate tones. Martin Price has called this vindication of satire "stylized." The speaker "has turned from artifice to naked honesty, from 'literature' to truth."[11] In this defense of satire, the satirist's voice is necessarily depersonalized and generalized. Thus Swift's poem begins with La Rochefoucauld's contentions about selfish man, proceeds to the particularly vicious examples of ego-satisfying reactions to the "death," and concludes with praise of Swift's selfless devotion to truth and morality, uttered by the "impartial" clubman at the Rose. But, of course, the "praise" is not "objective," nor does it constitute Swift's "real" view more than any other assumed point of view in the poem. That Swift actually believed many of the things the clubman asserts does not compromise the dramatic validity of his satiric strategy. As in the typical *débat* which takes place in the middle of Section IX (Digression on Madness) of *A Tale of a Tub*, Swift here plays out the fiction by means of critical irony that permits him a detached view of mortality.

Thus the developing satiric structure is reinforced by the underlying elegiac pattern of movement discernible in the poem. Swift the elegist, no less than Swift the satirist, expresses a particular view of reality by means of artful contrivance and rhetorical manipulation. Even in his most cynical moods, Swift formalizes feeling into art through the transforming agency of the elegiac imagination, pitting the idealizations of art against the experiences of time and loss. For Swift, then, the operations of time and fact of mortality bring paradoxically to life the creative imagination which fixes into the permanence of form this resistance to temporal reality. There is even the suggestion, in burlesque reversal of conventional elegiac feeling and tone, that the "dead" Swift is really not dead at all:

> "For when we open'd him we found
> That all his vital Parts were sound." (175-76)

The poet-speaker seems very much alive by being "dead." In this twist of elegiac sentiment, the literary anatomy being performed in the elegy establishes an indestructible poetic identity. But what is indestructible — the poem — finally expresses the idea that the poet and his art are subject to time. And recognition of the limits

11. *To the Palace of Wisdom: Studies in Order and Energy from Dryden to Blake* (Garden City: Doubleday, 1964), p. 164.

of art's truth characterizes the peculiar pathos of formal elegy. In the individual's experience of it, art rejoins reality.

Such tensions provide the basic dialectic between the ideal and real, art and life in Swift's poem. Thus satire is directed against the ambition to win public fame and fortune in these well-known lines:

Where's now this Fav'rite of *Apollo?*
Departed; *and his Works must follow:*
Must undergo the common Fate;
His Kind of Wit is out of Date. (249-52)

The lines present a negative view of poetry as a defense against time, but in a style utterly conventional and good-humored.[12] The elegist's detachment represents his attempt both to make poetry out of his hopeless circumstance and to cope with time through art.

Compared with this acknowledgment of mortality, the eulogist's emphatic language of permanence, which characterizes the final section of the poem, might seem a good example of Swiftian irony. The panegyrical shrillness culminates in the famous ringing judgment offered of Swift's place in history and literature:

"He gave the little Wealth he had,
To build a House for Fools and Mad:
And shew'd by one satyric Touch,
No Nation wanted it so much:
That Kingdom he hath left his Debtor,
I wish it soon may have a Better." (479-84)

The style and manner of praise is clearly exaggerated and extreme, comprising the tone of vain assertiveness informing those idealizations of the eulogist's imagination. The fierce rhetoric creates this illusion of permanence which is the consolation of elegy.

Exaggerations, whether hyperbole or understatement, are the staple of Swiftian rhetoric, and the eulogist's praise serves to point up the consciously stylized and literary quality of elegiac

12. cf. Fischer's reading of this passage, which stresses "the corruptibility of all worldly things" (p. 435). I am in substantial agreement with Fischer's reading here and elsewhere. But his is an essentially orthodox Christian interpretation, emphasizing providential compensations for mortality through love and charity, not those associated with the redemptive or restorative aspects of art itself, as I argue.

emotion. None of the perspective created in the structure is necessarily true and objective or false and ironical. They are the totality
of the poem's fiction. The sentiments are contrived and artificially
stimulated — resulting in the essential theatricality of the elegy. In
their helpful study of both textual and interpretive problems of
"Verses," Arthur Scouten and Robert Hume make a similar point:
"Every speaker... including Swift in the first person — has pro-
jected an *artificial* point of view. That is, we are not meant to
accept any statements as literally true."[13] But since the subject of
"Verses" is time and death, the speaker "controls" death by
imagining his own and shaping it into art. Although he may merely
entertain views toward his death, as he writes, Swift is acting upon
these views. Yet Swift takes his poem seriously enough not to
claim it as a surrogate for reality, and thus ultimately to trivialize
his art.

Swift considered death to be life's most tragic moment. As
he wrote to Mrs. Moore in 1727, "Life is a Tragedy, wherein we sit
as Spectators awhile, and then act our own Part in it."[14] The

13. "Pope and Swift: Text and Interpretation of Swift's Verses on His
Death," *PQ*, 52 (1973), 225. See also Edward W. Said, "Swift's Tory
Anarchy", *ECS*, 3 (1969), 48 -66. He describes Swift's mistrust and fear of
language and fictions, and his attempts to compensate by translating himself
into an "event in history." On "Verses" he says the following: "Swift's
death ... occurs in conversation, in language — nowhere else. Neither the
reader nor the poet can penetrate beyond the verbal dimension, which is the
imposition of a human standard upon nature. ... Thus even so serious and
natural a subject as death cannot be treated except as a function of language:
hence the unashamed artificiality of the poet's stage directions and shifting of
scene by which death is literally arranged. It becomes Swift's problem then to
show language as the arena in which fictions battle each other until only the
most worthy remain. And what remains of Swift can only be described, a
long time later, by an impartial, anonymous voice" (p. 64). I have no quarrel
with Said's general argument *except* for his erroneous contention that the
clubman's voice, purged of all bias, gives an objective and therefore true
account of Swift's "presence" as a writer in history who sees himself as too
honest and moral for his corrupted age. See also Ronald Paulson, *The
Fictions of Satire* (Baltimore: John Hopkins Press, 1967), pp. 189 -206, for
emphasis similar to Said's.
14. *Correspondence*, III, p. 254. This letter reads like a prose version of
the poem's argument.

diction and imagery are revealing, if conventionally Augustan for such matters. Swift's "Verses" is that tragic play; for he encounters the spectacle of his own death from the vantage point of director, actor, and spectator. He manipulates the stage action, participates in it, and watches it unfold before him. Like his famous countryman and admirer two centuries later, Swift appears to triumph over death: "Gaiety transfiguring all that dread" in the ideality of art. Like Yeats's own director-actor-spectator of "Lapis Lazuli," Swift has fused ideal and real, fiction and fact, art and life. Through art he has "died" and therefore achieved in that art the permanent and ultimate reality of life — his mortality. He has become the image of himself depicted in art. But as elegiac consolation this achievement is doubly ironic: rather than a comforting illusion of permanence, the image realized in art is not transcendent, but recalls the limits of that art as a meaningful alternative to time and mortality. As always, Swift refuses to be deluded, and rejects "the possession of being well deceived" either in his attitudes toward mortality or toward his art.

Chapter Six

Unlike his *Elegy,* to whose sentiments every bosom seems to return an echo, Gray's other poems, with few exceptions, have never been highly regarded. Recent years have seen a new interest in these poems and in Gray's position in literary history. This revaluation has taken two main courses: the literary historian puzzles over Gray's curiously divided poetic consciousness, one part Augustan, the other part romantic,[1] while the critic is now challenging the attacks on the language and structure of Gray's poetry, stemming from the objections of Wordsworth to the poetic diction.

Geoffrey Tillotson has pointed out that the alleged poetic diction Wordsworth censured in the sonnet to West is in fact dramatic: "for though it is himself who is speaking, [Gray] speaks by means of quotations from others."[2] Thus Gray's rejection of the artificial diction in his own sonnet underscores the sincerity of his grief, a grief too personal to be expressed in another poet's words. The borrowings Gray rejects are, interestingly enough, largely found in the descriptions of Eden in Milton's *Paradise Lost,* as Joseph Foladare has shown.[3] More recently, F. Doherty has viewed Gray's language as reflecting two distinctive voices: one public and highly decorative in style; the other private and straightforward in style.[4] Proceeding from Doherty's two categories, Patricia Meyer Spacks, in a significant and valuable essay on Gray's poems of 1742, suggests that his characteristic alternations between different types of artifice and more direct expression provide the structure and meaning of "Ode to Spring," the sonnet to West, and the Eton ode.[5] Citing Gray's "contrasting modes of

1. See Graham Hough, *The Romantic Poets* (London: Hutchinson's University Library, 1953), p. 13, for this typical view. The text used is *The Complete Poems of Thomas Gray* (Oxford: Clarendon Press, 1966), p. 92.
2. *Augustan Studies* (London: Athlone Press, 1961), p. 88. Wordsworth's objections to the sonnet are found in his preface to *Lyrical Ballads* (1800).
3. "Gray's 'Frail Memorial' to West," *PMLA,* 75 (1960), 61 -65.
4. "Two Voices of Gray," *Essays in Criticism,* 13 (1963), 222 -30.
5. "Statement and Artifice in Thomas Gray," *SEL,* 5 (1965), 519 -32.

poetry as a technique of cross-commentary," Mrs. Spacks rightly sees the theme of the sonnet as the limitations of art in expressing sincere emotion and personal grief.[6] There are, however, both practical and theoretical difficulties in her assertions, and some qualification, perhaps correction, is in order.

The case in point is the "Sonnet on the Death of Richard West," in which a contrast is apparent between the so-called sincere and direct expression of grief in lines 5-8 and 13-14 and the artificial rhetoric of lines 1-4 and 9-12, expressing the unity of man and nature and "the beauty and unity of the natural world."[7] The organization of contrasts, Mrs. Spacks argues, indicates that "the poet as artificer cannot merely through convention communicate the sorrow of the poet as man." While not entirely denying the idea of permanence through art, Gray seems to reject the artful and turn to a simpler, more direct expression of emotions. Such a reading of the sonnet, perceptive and sensitive as it is, creates a number of problems, not the least being what constitutes poetic sincerity.

Two main points confront the reader attempting to distinguish between artificial rhetoric and poetic sincerity: how relevant is the Miltonic context to Gray's allusions made in the sonnet; and how artless and direct are the lines Wordsworth approved in the poem? Such an investigation can provide a tentative answer as to whether Gray simply rejects artifice for direct statement or whether he sees the ordering of experience through art as insight into reality.

It is not difficult to see why the eighteenth-century elegist finds in *Paradise Lost* not only the basic philosophical and emotional conflicts at the heart of elegy, but also certain stylistic features appropriate to a formal expression of grief. Milton's epic framework treats man's fall from innocence and timelessness into the knowledge of time, loss, and death. To emphasize his sense of the loss, Gray borrowed diction and phraseology from the books dealing with the lost pastoral world of Eden. The language of these books of *Paradise Lost* is also appropriate to Gray's sonnet because of the feelings of loss it evokes. This pastoralism, literary and artificial as it is, depicts a unified world of ordered relation-

6. Spacks, p. 526.
7. Spacks, p. 527.

ships no longer available to the speaker in Gray's poem. But the reminders of that unavailability are built into the passages Gray borrows from. His rejection of this pastoralism is not, it can be shown, a superficial rejection based on the speaker's alienation from nature.[8]

An example of Milton's complication of attitude in Eden occurs in the famous evening hymn of Book IV:

> Now came still Ev'ning on, and Twilight gray
> Had in her sober Livery all things clad;
> Silence accompanied, for Beast and Bird,
> They to thir grassy Couch, these to thir Nests
> Were slunk, all but the wakeful Nightingale;
> She all night long her amorous descant sung;
> Silence was pleas'd: now glow'd the Firmament
> With living Sapphires: *Hesperus* that led
> The starry Host, rode brightest, till the Moon
> Rising in clouded Majesty, at length
> Apparent Queen unveil'd her peerless light,
> And o'er the dark her Silver Mantle threw. (598-609)

This is one of Milton's magnificent set-pieces, but it is not merely descriptive. Within the passage is a complex pattern of contrasting images. The recurrence of "now" underscores the theme of time in Eden, where the changing lights and darks and all other movements symbolize permanence and order underlying the cycles of nature. The incantatory effects produced by the repetition of "all," with its combination of pleasing labials and soothing assonance, along with the formalized simplicity of the diction suggest the ritual celebration of ordered variety in pastoral Eden. The verbs of the passage all involve opposed motions within the whole rotation of nature. The images of a breathlessly quiet night are contrasted with the glorious picture of the moon and stars piercing through and illuminating the darkness. In general, the first half of

---

8. Cf. Frank Brady, "Gray's *Elegy*: Structure and Meaning," *From Sensibility to Romanticism – Essays presented to Frederick A. Pottle*, eds. F. W. Hilles and H. Bloom (New York: Oxford University Press, 1965), pp. 177-89. Brady's brief discussion of "perspective" in Gray's poetry is helpful, but one problem with his specific point on Gray's "alienation" from nature in the sonnet to West is that the nature depicted there is not the nature of nineteenth-century romanticism, but a literary, artificial, and thus symbolic pastoralism.

the passage depicts the action of nature leading to nightfall and the second half the counteraction of the stars and moon in lighting up the blackness. This evening hymn contains contrasting opposites which in their basic circulatory motions establish Milton's theme of divine unity within movement and variety.[9]

The morning hymn that begins Book V of *Paradise Lost* completes the night-day cycle begun in Book IV:

> Now Morn her rosy steps in th'Eastern Clime
> Advancing, sow'd the Earth with Orient Pearl. (1-2)

At the end of this apostrophe to morning, Adam speaks to Eve at the moment she wakes: "Awake, the morning shines and the fresh field / Calls us" (20-21). The passage is clearly a blend of conventional references to morning, symbolizing renewal of the generative forces in the universe. The imagery emphasizes the "Perpetual Circle" of "ceaseless change," which is Milton's way of indicating the paradisal state of nature as an attitude of mind. But like the night hymn of Book IV, these lines reflect the ambiguity inherent in the setting: real darkness has just passed, Satan has already outlined the details of the temptation, and Eve has experienced her first disturbed night of sleep. The actions of seeding and fertilizing, implicit in the imagery of the passage, are already threatened by the destructive force of Eve's sterilizing pride. The symbolic associations of morning are therefore qualified in the larger context of the poem. And this morning hymn to ordered movement and permanent renewal also contains reminders of change, loss, and death, showing that the original Eden cannot last.

Gray employs two related types of allusive imagery to make connections between the world of Milton's Eden and his sonnet: one type is the direct use of a word or phrase from Milton, like the phrase "amorous Descant" from Book IV or "morning shines" (Gray pluralizes "morning") from Book V; the other type is a by-product of the direct reference: an evocation of a more general context from Milton that somehow relates to the speaker's world.

---

9. See Anne Davidson Ferry, *Milton's Epic Voice – The Narrator in "Paradise Lost"* (Cambridge, Mass.: Harvard University Press, 1963), p. 156. She points out that repetition and recurrence are Milton's structural method for depicting the ordered variety and idealized relationship of Eden.

Gray makes use of the many complications of attitude already operative in *Paradise Lost,* and reflects them through contrasts within his own sonnet structure. The reference to the birds' "Descant" at the beginning of Gray's poem,

> In vain to me the smileing Mornings shine,
> And redning Phoebus lifts his golden Fire:
> The Birds in vain their amorous Descant joyn;
> Or chearful Fields resume their green Attire. (1-4)

suggests the nightingale's song in the evening hymn singled out by Milton's narrator, which traditionally stands for the function of the poetic imagination in awakening human consciousness, even when the subject is darkness and death. As Joseph Summers points out, in *Paradise Lost* "the nightingale . . . is always . . . the singer of fulfilled love."[10] Such fulfillment contrasts with the sorrow of Gray's speaker growing out of his experience with death. Thus the birds' "Descant" only accentuates the speaker's loss of the shared joys of mutual literary endeavor."[11]

A similar complicating effect can be seen in Gray's borrowing of "morning shines" from Book V. Milton's phrase occurs within the continuous patterning of day-night and recurring seasonal change emblematic of the harmony and order of the timeless world of Eden. But to the grief-stricken speaker the diurnal round of nature exemplifies the transitory nature of all things. Depending on the speaker's state of mind, repetition and recurrence in the natural world can symbolize pattern within order, change within permanence, or the reality of disorder and death. But in his cry "in vain" the speaker is not simply rejecting the pastoral world, idealized and remote; like Milton's Eden, which often depicts the unfallen world by means of pastoral imagery derived from the fallen world, the pastoral world of the sonnet acknowledges in its very denial both the idealized world

10. Joseph Summers, *The Muse's Method: An Introduction to "Paradise Lost"* (Cambridge, Mass.: Harvard University Press, 1962), p. 98.

11. See *Correspondence of Thomas Gray*, ed. P. Toynbee and L. Whibley (Oxford: Clarendon Press, 1935), I *passim*. In their letters West and Gray often exchanged poems and comments on these poems and on literature in general. These letters would, also, often make reference to a Greek or Latin poet and some contemporary writer.

and the actual world of time and therefore of death. The "Joys" in the speaker's breast are indeed "imperfect," as are all literary paradises.

Once one is aware of the allusory mode of the sonnet, he can better understand the function of these references transformed by Gray into the fabric of his own verse. The ambiguities are rich in the phrases "smileing Mornings" (1) and "chearful Fields" (4). In the process of denying the possibility of renewal, the speaker is acknowledging it. For, as he admits, the mornings smile and the fields are cheerful. In this case, denial acts as a form of assertion. What seems to be contradictory in the language of lines 1 and 4 is actually the paradox inherent in the elegiac view. The ambivalence expressed toward death in the elegy establishes a balance between the ideal and the actual. The achievement of this balance can be seen in the speaker's change of attitudes from a view of death as senseless to a view of death as somehow tolerable — as in the personal meditations of the elegist in *Lycidas* or in Shelley's *Adonais* or in a speaker's objective presentation of the tensions generated by the resistance to, yet acceptance of, death as part of life — as in Augustan elegy.

Lines 9-12 of the sonnet are a variation on lines 1-4, and one finds there are many of the same words as in 1-4: "birds" and "fields" recur; the phrase "smileing Mornings shine" becomes "Morning Smiles"; "chearful" changes to "chear"; other men ("the busy Race") respond to nature in contrast to the bereaved speaker, who cannot respond to the world depicted in lines 1-4. This sameness of language emphasizes the speaker's loss of a pastoral world. The action depicted in the verbs in these lines and the repetition of diction from lines 1-4 suggest the timeless motion which characterized the ideal pastoral world of lines 1-4:

> Yet Morning Smiles the busy Race to chear,
> And new-born Pleasure brings to happier Men:
> The Fields to all their wonted Tribute bear:
> To warm their little Loves the Birds complain. (9-12)

In line 10, for example, Gray adopts this idea of birth from the fertilization metaphors found in Milton's morning hymn of Book V. The constant renewal of nature in Gray's term "new-born" suggests the perpetual creativity within a timeless state, except to his speaker, for whom it suggests the opposite — death. The phrase "new-born Pleasure" thus operates ironically, since the new day of lines 1 and 9 ultimately brings to the speaker thoughts of death. The phrase "happier Men" also suggests its opposite when the grieving speaker implicitly compares himself to those oblivious to his grief.

The repetition of words, the borrowings from Milton's pastoral scenes, and the stylized imagery Gray fashions in lines 1-4 and 9-12 evoke the ceremonial and iterative qualities so appropriate to the ritualistic elements in elegy itself. A phrase like "redning Phoebus lifts his golden fire," which Coleridge censured as redundant, assigns to Phoebus the priestlike role of offering himself as the sacrament of poetic inspiration. The phrase "resume their green Attire" depicts the field in the formal gesture of putting on an article of clothing, much like Milton's twilight that clothes all things "in her sober Livery" (IV, 599). And the phrasing of "The Fields to all their wonted Tribute bear" clearly implies the ritual of strewing flowers, a conventional mark of tribute to the dead.

References to Milton, it can be seen, are therefore as functional for an Augustan elegist as allusions to the classical epic are for the Augustan satirist. They are not simply mechanical comparisons but active metaphors, depending often for their effects on traditional literary associations. Instead of disvaluing, as the satirist does by juxtaposing the epic ideal with the contemporary scene, Gray generates a wider and more complex elegiac context by relating the Miltonic elements to the situation of his own sonnet. This allusiveness, moreover, gives the sonnet its distinctive Augustan quality.

The conventional pastoral imagery in lines 1-4 and 9-12 has a stylized, literary quality about it, not necessarily because much of it is borrowed from Milton's pastoral scenes, but largely because Gray is writing in a highly personal manner. Understanding the function of the Miltonic context in Gray's sonnet is important but should not be overemphasized; it is just as important to recognize that this pastoralism is *not* Milton's, but Milton's filtered through Gray's sensibility. It is true that change, loss, and death and the desire to lament these conditions are permanent features of the human situation. But Gray alters conventional language to fit his own particular needs. The stylized quality of the sonnet's imagery is the speaker's way of shaping his ambivalent attitude toward loss and death.

The imaginative ideal embodied in the pastoralism is attractive and forceful, and the fact that this ideal is depicted in eight lines out of fourteen indicates its central meaning for the poem. Unlike the romantic elegist, who depicts loss and and sorrow in positive images and metaphors, Gray expresses his sorrow indirectly by contrasting his particular state of mind with that represented in the pastoral ideal. The speaker's perspective changes in respect to this pastoralism, but the imagery persists. The pastoral figures involve process, movement, and change implied in the day-night cycles and the seasonal changes. But process is paradoxically depicted here by static set-pieces. The effect is something like that which Keats creates in describing the Grecian urn: what is depicted on the surface is changeless because lifeless; or, to rephrase it in elegiac terms, deathless because lifeless. Gray's fixing of these recurring motions of nature into the confines of the sonnet form cannot, however, compensate for the despair and anguish brought into the world by the reality of death. The speaker's imagination, the only weapon he has in his struggle with time, has finally only a limited effectiveness against the fact of mortality. This limitation is the real subject of the sonnet.

The achievement of permanence through art seems illusory to the speaker confronted with the facts of time and death. Milton's Christian solution to these facts is not relevant for Gray. No such theological resolution is possible.[12] Even the creative imagination provides little solace. In fact, the ineffectuality of the artist's act of idealization, his basic defense against time, is what the grieving speaker acknowledges metaphorically in lines 1-4 and 9-12, and what, in lines 13-14, he refers to directly. By depicting these pastoral scenes in such formal and stylized images, he is admitting their attractiveness, recognizing the sense of beauty and artistic satisfaction associated with any ordering of things, but at the same time admitting that what they depict is essentially unreal and illusory.

In the sonnet the speaker's complex attitude as revealed in lines 1-4 finds its expression in the negation of life symbols, including renewal in nature and poetic creativity. Yet in having the

12. There is the possibility of an ambiguity in the word "him" of line 13, "I fruitless mourn to him, that cannot hear," which could possibly refer either to West or to Milton's God, implying for Gray the failure of traditional Christian consolation and hope.

speaker view his sorrow through the absence of positives, Gray both accentuates the void caused by their nonexistence and implies that they are possible, but only as imaginative projections. Consequently, by rejecting the processes of nature as fixed in a verbal construct, the speaker both rejects the illusion of an idealized defense against the destruction of time and underscores his own finiteness and consciousness of time.

In determining how the speaker's attitudes change from his feeling of inconsolable loss in lines 1-4 to his total hopelessness and futility in lines 9-14, the kind of linkage provided by lines 5-8 must be examined. These lines function dramatically in the sonnet and indicate the precise reasons for the speaker's deepening despair between lines 1-4 and 9-12. But to call this linkage flat and lacking metaphorical density when compared with lines 1-4 and 9-12, as Foladare does, is to mistake difference for badness.[13]

These lines differ from 1-4 and 9-12, and also from the assertion of 13-14:

These Ears, alas! for other Notes repine,
A different Object do these Eyes require.
My lonely Anguish melts no Heart, but mine;
And in my Breast the imperfect Joys expire. (5-8)

If there is relaxation here, one should decide whether this relaxation fits both the speaker's state of mind at the moment and the developing line of emotion in the sonnet. The word "alas" is more than merely an exclamation; it indicates hesitation, a dramatic breaking off before the crescendo to the heavily accented word "other" (5), a word that emphasizes the ineffectuality of the "Object," or stylized imagery of lines 1-4.

There are other obvious links between lines 5-8 and 1-4. "Ears" and "Notes" revert to the birds' amorous descant, now unheard. "Eyes" brings to mind the striking visual quality of the pastoral figures in 1-4. Being unable to respond through these two senses, the speaker underscores the numbing effect of his sorrow. The word "repine" means literally to languish in one's discontent and is a precise description of the speaker's state of mind at this point. "Expire" means to breathe out, or, often, to die, and

13. "Gray's 'Frail Memorial' to West", p. 63.

reminds the reader of the mortality which is the reason for "imperfect Joys." The word "imperfect" sends the reader back to the Eden of 1-4 and ahead to 9-12, where the built-in qualifications of Milton's Eden are reflected through Gray's imagery.

The emptiness and negation experienced by the speaker are presented directly in these lines. To dramatize the "lonely Anguish" or the "imperfect Joys" would work against the whole drift of the poem. The speaker's explanations in lines 5-8 cannot be made positive without diluting the unrelieved negation which causes his desperate reaching for "a different Object." An emphatic rendering of the speaker's sorrow in the figured style of the preceding or following lines would destroy the alternating rise and fall of emotional intensities expressed in this sonnet. Despite Wordsworth's claim to the contrary, lines 5-8 are not "the language of prose," but are in fact poetic, emphasizing the denotative meaning in contrast to the symbolic associations of lines 1-4 and 9-12. The difference between these lines and lines 1-4 and 9-12 lies in the tone of despair that characterizes this middle portion of the sonnet. The speaker views his situation in a voice less self-consciously allusive and in the accents of the repeated first-person pronouns. The change of time relates to the other quatrains of the sonnet and functions meaningfully in the total context. The feelings in lines 5-8 are strong but subdued, and they prepare for the main issue treated in lines 13-14 of the sonnet.

Lines 9-12 mark the speaker's final but futile acknowledgment of the pastoral ideal. The speaker's return to the highly stylized expression of these lines emphasizes his frustration that others respond to a world alien to him. The speaker's hopelessness, nevertheless, turns him back on himself, and he faces directly in the final lines the problem all elegists eventually must face:

> I fruitless mourn to him, that cannot hear,
> And weep the more, because I weep in vain. (13-14)

As Foladare has argued, the word "fruitless" is especially appropriate as an expression of the failure of the fructifying influence of West as friend and poet.[14] Wordsworth objected to the grammar of "fruitless," asserting that it flawed the line. But the equivocal syntax of the word is meaningful: "fruitless," seeming to act as

14. Foladare, p. 63.

both appositive and adverb, creates one of the significant tensions in the speaker's final attitude. He has reached the extremities of grief because he has been cut off from West and from any joy in the fulfillment of their mutual literary interests. His poem is, in the final analysis, unsatisfactory as consolation. He has abandoned the conventions of pastoral. In addition, his despair is deepened because it seems inexpressible; therefore, his situation and its causes are brought together simultaneously in the ambiguous syntax.

The simplicity and directness of these final lines, presumably free from all stylized diction, brought praise from Wordsworth and perhaps account for descriptions of the poem as "heartfelt," or as characterized by "simple sincerity and depth of feeling."[15] The lines appear to be unadorned statement, marking a change in style and emphasis from the pastoralism of lines 1-4 and 9-12 and from the direct expression of the speaker's grief in lines 5-8. And these lines reveal the speaker's turning away from his poeticizing in lines 1-12 to a specific consideration of his role as elegist and of the function of elegiac poetry. He is viewing the implications of what he has just performed in the preceding lines.

Though different in style, the lines are carefully tied to the rest of the poem. The repetition of "I," the recurrence of the phrase "in vain" (uttered three times in fourteen lines, and two of these in beginning and ending the sonnet) establish by insistent refrain the hopelessness of the situation for the speaker-poet. If these lines fall prey to sentimental lingering and indulgence, then the sonnet is vulnerable to the charge of being "heartbroken," reflecting the poet's inability to relate his personal loss to the wider ramifications of the universal human condition.[16] If these lines say only that the speaker weeps "in vain" because his lament is "in vain," the poem circles around the dead center of a neurotic self-absorption, and the claim for Gray's romanticism may be

15. Lord David Cecil, "Poetry of Thomas Gray," in *Eighteenth-Century Literature,* ed. James L. Clifford (New York: Oxford University Press, 1959), p. 247. See also R. D. Havens, *The Influence of Milton on English Poetry* (Cambridge, Mass.: Harvard University Press, 1922), p. 491.

16. R. W. Ketton-Cremer, *Thomas Gray – A Biography* (Cambridge: University Press, 1955), p. 64.

justified. The poem is then static, and it contains no resolution of its conflicts.

When the speaker refers to West's death in terms of the dying out of all joyousness in song, he is recognizing the fact of mutability, not indulging in self-pity: "And in my Breast the imperfect Joys expire" (8). But the "expiring," or breathing out, connects with the idea of weeping, emphasized by the repetition in the last line, of "weep" and relating directly to the elegist's expression of grief: "And weep the more, because I weep in vain" (14). The repetition of "weep" metaphorically suggests the persistence of grief for the speaker. The direct expression of lines 13-14 creates its own ironic context: the reader hears only too well, as does the grief-stricken speaker, what is intended for the unhearing West.

The turning from general considerations of loss and of death to the question of death as it especially affects the poet and his poetry is standard practice in the Augustan elegy. For instance, the speaker in Gray's *Elegy* is not unmindful of future judgments of his elegiac efforts. He speculates at length on the idea of artistic permanence, even to the point of imagining his own epitaph.[17] Gray's sonnet, however, maintains the characteristic Augustan acceptance of man's finiteness along with the possibility of preserving his memory in artifice.

In most elegies the speaker's experience with and analysis of time and death bring him to some kind of understanding and acceptance of his own situation. Usually these discoveries involve recognition of an enduring value in the human struggle itself, especially in the poet's creation of the poem, with its own independent life, out of a world of change and death. The elegist's struggle during his poem to make sense out of death mirrors every man's common concern with mortality. Thus, as Gray's speaker explores this basic dilemma facing all men, he discovers what can ameliorate the reality of time and death. The result of this process

17. Cf. Brady, p. 187: It is the "Narrator's elegy . . . not a general threnody, and resignation is balanced by self-realization." In comparing the form and emphasis of Gray's *Elegy* with the ordinary Augustan elegiac expression, Brady tends to see differences. But the Augustan elegy, like all others, is ultimately a narrator's or speaker's elegy, as my argument tries to show.

is the poem as object, a structure of meanings which formalizes the act of discovery. The finished poem is also the elegist's memorial from the living to the dead, despite the speaker's claim that it is an ineffective tribute. The last lines reflect this paradox between what the poem says and what it is:

> I fruitless mourn to him, that cannot hear,
> And weep the more, because I weep in vain. (13-14)

The speaker seems to call out against the idea that poetry can conquer time or fix past associations into something permanent. In formalizing his feelings as a poet, the speaker, despite his protests to the contrary or perhaps because of his protests, acknowledges art as a "mythic" defense against time, to use Thomas Edwards's term in describing Pope's view of art in his Augustan poems.[18] Though cast entirely as negative protest, the final lines imply a positive view of the creative act. From the beginning the sonnet continually affirms and refutes, asserts and qualifies by using the ready-made ambiguities in the Milton passages, mediated through Gray's own structure.

The speaker ends as he begins — by accounting for the many contradictions of a given view. The negative conclusion of his lament turns out to be a positive assertion that art redeems time by being an arrangement of materials into significant form. The poem as verbal construct expresses the ineffectuality of mourning; but instead of contradicting itself, it turns out to be, as an act of tribute and remembrance, a consolation in spite of itself. Thus, imaginative idealizations of past joy, fulfillment, and creativity survive only in the poem that laments their loss. (There is the hint that the speaker has in mind not only his loss of a friend but, in his references to Milton, perhaps the loss of a great age of poetry.) What remains of past associations are the memories eternalized in art. What remains of a past age of poetry is what the poet has salvaged and made part of his own idiom. Yet this transformation

---

18. *This Dark Estate: A Reading of Pope,* Perspectives in Criticism No. 11 (Berkeley and Los Angeles: University of California Press, 1963), p. 12, Edwards sees Pope's early poems as demonstrating a balance between "myths of permanence" and "ideas of time's finality." The informing structural feature of the Augustan elegy is a similar balance between symbols of life, permanence, and order, and those of death, loss, and chaos.

brings little gain and emphasizes the inevitable loss: the **basic** theme of elegiac poetry.

The speaker's paradoxical disclaimer yet assertion of the value of poetry in lines 13-14 — prepared for earlier by his expression of complex attitudes toward art, loss, and death — receives full dramatization in the structural ironies that compose the sonnet's meaning. These ironies involve relationships between external factors and internal matters of the sonnet: Gray's choice of the sonnet form itself instead of the conventional pastoral elegy or public ode may be indirect recognition of Milton's debt to the Italian sonnet; nevertheless, it clashes with a reader's "stock" expectations in the situation. The allusions to *Paradise Lost* recall the pastoral scenes of Milton's Eden. Gray's tight, rigidly metrical, and regularly rhymed sonnet reduces the sweep of Milton's blank verse, while permitting the speaker to express a complex attitude toward death. The personal quality of the grief contrasts with the detachment and distance achieved by the stylized "literary" imagery. First-person references contrast with the generalized diction; the speaker's intellectual struggle exists side by side with his carefully modulated emotional struggle; the assertions claiming the futility of art as a consolation are qualified by the consoling effects of elegy as ritual. Gray's "Sonnet on the Death of Richard West" comes close to fulfilling the demands of the ideal Augustan poem, "one in which maximum tension has resulted from a struggle of contraries of many kinds."[19]

19. Maynard Mack, "Alexander Pope," *Major British Writers,* ed. G. B. Harrison (New York: Harcourt, Brace and World, 1959), p. 754.

Chapter Seven

"Nature and reason have dictated to every nation," said Samuel Johnson in 1740 about epitaph writing, "that to preserve good actions from oblivion, is both the interest and duty of mankind." The Augustan age of English literature provides ample illustration of this elegiac impulse to "preserve" and sustain, noted by Johnson, in the universal commitment to the kind of literary performance that rescues man's accomplishment from oblivion by redeeming time through the permanence of art. Works as different as Boswell's *Life of Johnson,* where human wit, intelligence, good fellowship, folly, even anger are immortalized and, Pope's *Dunciad,* where both classical and Christian intellectual traditions are perpetuated ironically through the mock order and sardonic parody of "Saturnian days of Lead and Gold," are moving testimony to this desire among the Augustans.

Johnson's own writings, ranging in style and intent from his *Preface* to the *Dictionary* to the great *Lives of the Poets,* though preoccupied with the problems of language and meaning, nevertheless affirm art's power to transform fact and truth into an ideal order by his very devotion to a life of writing.

Although brief, the highly praised and moving "On the Death of Dr. Robert Levet" (1783) clearly exemplifies this conflict between time and art which characterizes Augustan elegiac writing. At first glance this description of the well-known elegy may seem at worst perverse and at best misleading, for Johnson's poem, in the words of one trusted critic of the period, "is the logical conclusion of the Augustan taste for truth to nature in style and subject."[1] Miss Trickett's assertions as to the poem's essential simplicity of style and directness of method are the result of some questionable assumptions about both Johnson and the poem — assumptions underlying the commonly-held viewpoint on this elegy as Johnson's "positive restatement and demonstration of his negative criticism" of the pastoral tradition in general and Milton's

1. Rachel Trickett, *The Honest Muse: A Study in Augustan Verse* (Oxford: Clarendon Press, 1967), p. 256.

Lycidas in particular.[2] In discussions of Johnson's critical opinions, the two elegies are invariably paired as opposites to make a point about Johnson's "sincerity" and dislike of fictions. But it is a mistake to view these poems as necessarily incompatible because their styles are so different. For if *Lycidas* represents Milton's "literary" depiction of grief, the Levet poem reveals on Johnson's part a total commitment to art and artifice in the same spirit of commitment to the moral imagination he demands in that difficult couplet near the end of *The Vanity of Human Wishes* :

> With these [values], celestial wisdom calms the mind,
> And makes the happiness she does not find.[3]

In life, Johnson is insisting on vigorous moral activism and on the creative role of the mind and intelligence; in art as well, he demonstrates a similar creative vigor and vivid realization of image and theme, which, while not visionary or prophetic, is truly professional and sophisticated.

If the vexing problem of "poetic sincerity" has detracted from the art of the Levet elegy, the tendency to view Johnson's writing against the background of his life and times as recorded by Boswell often diverts the reader from essential critical analysis. In the case of Dr. Levet we are blessed with a biographical void. The inconclusive reports of Boswell and Hawkins, and the "anonymous" character sketch of Levet published in the *Gentleman's Magazine* of February 1785 share the puzzlement one feels over the patent incongruity of background, talents, and habits of the two men. Perhaps we can do no better than to settle for Hawkins's terse comment: "He [Levet] had no learning, and consequently was an unfit companion for a learned man."[4] We are happily forced, therefore, to restrict our reading to the verbal and imagistic matters at hand.[5]

2. See Bertrand H. Bronson, "Personification Reconsidered," in *Facets of the Enlightenment: Studies in English Literature and Its Contexts* (Berkeley: University of California Press, 1968), p. 120.

3. *The Poems of Samuel Johnson,* eds. D. N. Smith and E. L. McAdam (Oxford: Clarendon Press, 1941), pp. 199-202. All quotations of Johnson's poems are from this edition.

4. Sir John Hawkins, *Life of Samuel Johnson, L.L.D.* (London: J. Buckland, 1787), p. 404.

5. Even in his excellent study of abstractions and personification in the

On close scrutiny Johnson's tribute turns out to be something of an elegiac variation on some familiar literary themes and conventions, as his Juvenalian imitations and *Rasselas,* to mention two obvious examples, surely are of their respective models. As Paul Fussell rightly points out, when lamenting Levet's death Johnson "betakes himself to the artificial mechanisms of stanza form and poetic diction, and he uses a meter deriving from previous poems rather than from the pulses of his heart."[6] And one could safely add that Johnson also uses materials deriving from earlier depictions of men of good works. Instead of being "superfluous" to "moral or psychological truth," as René Wellek has insisted,[7] Johnson's art is his method of confronting as well as coping with the reality of time. To rephrase the often misread conundrum of the elegy ("The power of art without the show," 16) often invoked to describe the poem's effect, the "power" of "On the Death of Dr. Robert Levet" resides in its imaginative ordering of grief and praise into a unique verbal structure that itself mediates between the idealization of art and the facts of time and mortality inspiring it.

In a particularly revealing comment, Johnson gives a clue to the artistic, if not personal, usefulness of Levet as subject matter of an elegiac poem. "Poor Levet," wrote Johnson, "died in his bed the other day by a sudden stroke; So uncertain are human things."[8] A commonplace to be sure, this statement nonetheless highlights a special Johnsonian mode of thought: the constant effort to connect the particular with the general, the real with the ideal, the original insight with the literary convention, and life with art. The remark also underscores the fundamental dialectical mode characterizing the elegiac imagination in mediating between the actual eighty-year-old "obscure practiser in physic" (Boswell's

Levet elegy and other eighteenth-century poems, Bronson tends to justify literary contrivance by claiming that contemporary readers would not have considered artifice as such, but rather as a vehicle of deeply felt emotion.

6. *Samuel Johnson and the Life of Writing* (New York: Harcourt Brace Jovanovich, 1971), pp. 54-55.

7. *A History of Modern Criticism: 1750-1950* (New Haven: Yale University Press, 1955), I, 79.

8. *The Letters of Samuel Johnson,* ed. R. W. Chapman (Oxford: Oxford University Press), II, 463.

phrase) and Levet as symbol, transformed by Johnson's imagination into a composite literary type who is an idealized blend of a stock eighteenth-century figure — the man of good works. In this "symbolic" Levet are vestiges of a literary and ethical tradition extending as far back as Horace, Virgil, and biblical parable, but existing as recently as the virtuous rustic praised in Gray's churchyard elegy and in Goldsmith's long poems.[9]

The interplay of these motifs displays itself in the following stanza describing Levet's medical ministry:

> No summons mock'd by chill delay,
> No petty gain disdain'd by pride,
> The modest wants of ev'ry day
> The toil of ev'ry day supplied. (21-24)

What might seem a simple metaphor to express the idea that Levet was prompt and dependable in treatment of patients, on closer examination, reveals the complex wit we have learned to expect from Augustan writers. Against the pervasive elegiac irony inherent in a lament, death, in this particular stanza, reverses roles with Levet, acting in fact as promptly as did the doctor in caring for the sick ("Death broke at once the vital chain," 35). This elegiac mood checks the idealizing praise of Levet's charity, since death, as often in its Renaissance characterization, assumes here a distinctly uncharitable role. In addition, the biblical echoes of another famous healer, Christ, the target of scornful taunts on Calvary, tends to elevate Levet's stature momentarily, while intensifying the ironic situation: "He saved others; himself he cannot save" (Mark 15:31). Levet, of course, is no Christ, and Johnson, who was generally skeptical of religious themes and references in poetry, would never risk his tone by such an absurd analogy; but there is the suggestion throughout the poem that Levet is the true servant of God, having employed well his "single talent" (28). In this sense Levet repeats in these humble ministerings a pattern of divine history: Christ's life and person as seen through the image of the great Physician, a familiar honorific association Pope uses easily and effectively in his tribute to Dr. Arbuthnot. For John-

9. See Trickett, esp. pp. 256-263. Although Miss Trickett acknowledges the existence of these traditions in Johnson's elegy, she does not show how they function in the poem.

son, as for Pope, such unpretentious devotion to human well-being was the ultimate Christian heroism.

Despite the honorific implications, verbal ambiguities qualify this conception of Levet as idealized Christian hero, gently reminding us of Levet's frailty and foibles as man. In line 22 "petty," as defined in Johnson's *Dictionary*, means "small" or "unimportant." Juxtaposed with the economic connotations of "gain," the phrase generates definite commercial overtones. Prideful men often scorn things not directly serving their immediate concerns and self-interest. However, Levet's selflessness makes him vulnerable to another kind of pride, the reverse of egoistic ambition and object of much Restoration and eighteenth-century satire — pettiness and gullibility stemming from lack of intellectual prudence and discrimination in human affairs. The praise is qualified here, but not harshly, and Johnson's shrewd intelligence is revealed in the speaker's acknowledgment of Levet's idiosyncrasies.

But the following biblical reference to the Parable of the Talents (Matthew 25:15) sets forth in clear terms the idealized portrait of Levet as Christian hero:

> His virtues walk'd their narrow round,
>   Nor made a pause, nor left a void;
> And sure th'Eternal Master found
>   The single talent well employ'd. (25-28)

In this stanza, of course, the situation is the opposite of that depicted negatively in the parable. For Johnson is saying that Levet has fulfilled Christ's directives and made excellent use of his one talent.[10] The extent and force of the speaker's approval are suggested dramatically by the positive praise which replaces the strong contempt expressed in the Matthew account.

Merging with this depiction of the ideal obedient servant of God is another biblical rendition of the man-of-good-works figure — the story of the Samaritan in Luke (11:30-37). Levet's characterization as

> Of ev'ry friendless name the friend (8)

makes him exemplary of a Christian love which defines all men as neighbors. In the larger scheme of salvation, as the speaker sees it,

10. See Susie Tucker and Henry Gifford, *Expl.* XV (1957), item 45.

Levet, like the Samaritan, ultimately serves God in such a way as to permit his participation in the final,redemptive phase of human history. Yet the plain diction, rhythmic simplicity, and undemonstrative quality of the verse indicate Johnson's studied refusal to heighten the poetry into praise of this friend of the friendless. Thus the idealizing impulses of elegiac poetry are qualified by style. Such restraint and economy of expression are cited as proof of Johnsonian realism and honesty. But they function here to effect an important balance of the dialectical oppositions between the ideal and the real Levet. Even the choice of the anonymous "name" to describe the doctor-patient relationship further reinforces, at the verbal level, the idea of Levet's selfless compassion for all men. Ideal and real coalesce in these unsuspecting lines, producing the characteristic tension of opposing forces which animates Augustan elegy.

These traits of simplicity and moral righteousness characterizing Levet in the poem are further developed in the rhetoric of the following two lines:

> The modest want of ev'ry day
> The toil of ev'ry day supplied. (23-24)

"Wants" leads easily into "toil," which in turn logically resolves in the notion of "supplied," the point at which we witness both idea and feeling of expectation fulfilled in the appropriate sense of relief implicit in the word "supplied." Moreover, as with any form of repetition, prose rhythms, reinforced by parallel phrasing, create measured movement, emphasizing here the dependability and routine nature of Levet's medical care. Sound not only echoes sense in the obvious way that Pope meant, but style itself imitates the ordered, harmonious Nature, "the source, and end, and test" of a truly moral act.

Whatever his personal emotions, Johnson is not capable of literary sentimentality, and the speaker's attitude toward Levet is always in control, despite the idealizations. Since Johnson is fully committed to the complexities inherent in the experience of time and loss, he guards against the type of "pure" elegizing which excludes the fullest possible range of elegiac emotions and interpretations of experience. Ironies lurk in the key terms used to describe Levet: "officious," "innocent," "sincere," and "well tried." It is just such ambiguity of attitude which is summed up in the one-line description of Levet of which T. S. Eliot was so fond — the man "obscurely wise, and coarsely kind." In the *Dictionary* Johnson defines "innocence" as purity (from Original Sin), freedom from guilt of one kind or another, and also a state of innocence and simplicity, "perhaps with some degree of weakness." To say that someone is "well tried" implies that he is experienced; but the meaning can suggest being abused and scorned, too, as Levet allegedly was. Although most modern editors read "officious" as "kind, doing good services," meanings related to the positive aspects of Levet's life, the definition Mrs. Thrale records in her *British Synonomy* mentions the favorable reading and also the meaning of "troublesome."[11] Thus, Johnson's praise of Levet activates a realistic intelligence which tests the idealizations against the sober actualities of experience.

The imagination-reality, art-life dialectic in connection with Levet's accomplishments is further developed through the image of the "open and ironic road," as Paul Fussell describes this familiar motif in Johnson and in other eighteenth-century writers.[12]

> His virtues walk'd their narrow round,
> Nor made a pause, nor left a void. (25-26)

Lecturing his sister, Nekayah, on the meager possibilities of happiness in this world, Rasselas speaks by means of similar words and images: "It is our business to consider what beings like us may perform; each labouring for his own happiness, by promoting within his circle, however narrow, the happiness of others." Dr. Levet's own "rounds" as general practitioner are a fitting illustration of Rasselas' definition of human virtue. "This confined circle of duty is remarkable for that unremarkable completeness, enemy to discontinuity," according to Murray Krieger.[12a]

But travel, as Johnson wrote to Mrs. Thrale of his trip to the Western Islands, "is to regulate imagination by reality" (September 21, 1773), and in the more somber elegy Johnson records the

11. Hester Thrale Piozzi, *British Synonomy* (Dublin: Porter, 1794), pp. 309-10.

12. *The Rhetorical World of Augustan Humanism: Ethics and Imagery from Swift to Burke* (Oxford: Clarendon Press, 1965), p. 264.

12a. *The Classic Vision: The Retreat from Extremity in Modern Literature* (Baltimore: John Hopkins Press, 1971), p. 143.

devastating victory of mortality, a sad triumph of nature over the practice of virtue itself, symbolized by the traditional circle of perfection and permanence. For a committed moralist like Johnson, the tragic irony generated reflects not only his constitutional pessimism but implicitly questions the efficacy of art as a viable defense against time. The metaphor provides a certain distance and objectivity; but even when the metaphoric formulation conceptually acknowledges the completeness and persistence of virtue ("Nor made a pause, nor left a void"), these virtues cannot ultimately defeat time. The "pause" and "void" emphasize only too well the feelings of loss and regret inherent in elegiac irony throughout the poem.

But the artist's capacity to fictionalize challenges the power of time and mortality. Johnson's imaginative conversion of the actual flesh-and-blood Levet into the symbolic man of good works provides for the survival of Levet in artistic permanence. His imagined self is a composite of various classical and Christian traditions which idealize the simple life, rural virtue, moral uprightness, and charitable works. Northrop Frye is right in his contention that in a poem what often passes as intensely personal sentiment is actually the poet's conscious reshaping of conventions and devices of an earlier literary tradition.[13]

Johnson's Levet owes as much to the commingling of literary traditions which inform Pope's aristocratic Man of Ross and the portrait of an unambitious father in the *Epistle to Dr. Arbuthnot,* and even to the obscure but virtuous rustics peopling Gray's *Elegy,* as to the facts of Levet's life. Like Pope himself, Johnson views individuals, such as the Dick Minims, Wolseys, King Charleses, as representations of a universal type, and sees them often through "the lens of a convention."[14]

"If Pope be not a poet," said Johnson, "where is poetry to be found? " His good-man portrait of Levet appears to show the influence of his poetic master:

Rise, honest Muse! and sing the Man of Ross.

(Moral Essay, III, 250)

13. *Anatomy of Criticism: Four Essays* (Princeton: Princeton University Press, 1957), p. 97.

14. See Maynard Mack, *The Garden and the City: Retirement and Politics in the Later Poetry of Pope 1731 -1743,* (Toronto: University of Toronto Press, 1969), p. 107.

The almost epic elevation here establishes the larger idealizing framework within which another familiar idealizing occurs:

> Is any sick? the Man of Ross relieves,
> Prescribes, attends, the med'cine makes,and gives. (269-70)

Consider in addition the quiet celebration of the elder Pope in *Dr. Arbuthnot*:

> Born to no Pride, inheriting no Strife,
> Nor marrying Discord in a Noble Wife,
> Stranger to Civil and Religious Rage,
> The good Man walk'd innoxious thro' his Age . . . .
> Un-learn'd,he knew no Schoolman's subtle Art,
> No language, but the Language of the Heart. (392-95; 398-99)

Combine with these sentiments the nostalgic moodiness of Gray's elegiac quatrain

> Far from the madding crowd's ignoble strife,
>   Their sober wishes never learn'd to stray;
> Along the cool sequester'd value of life
>   They kept the noiseless tenor of their way (73-76)

and we sense the literary resonance behind Johnson's characterization of Levet. Deleting what is inappropriate for elegy, the Johnson version naturally omits the heroic strain of Pope and the rural nostalgia of Gray. Nevertheless, this image of Levet achieves imaginative reality through the impact of a familiar literary ancestry. While not corresponding in all details to the Horatian and Popean ideal of country life, or to Gray's version of pastoral innocence, still the active moralist who emerges in the portrait represents aspects of these simple virtues and traditional pieties Johnson clearly found morally exemplary and emotionally appealing:

> Yet still he fills affection's eye,
>   Obscurely wise, and coarsely kind;
> Nor letter'd arrogance deny
>   The praise to merit unrefin'd. (9-12)

Differing as this does from Pope's and Gray's lines in both rhythm and accent, Johnson's stanza does, however, share the ideas and sentiments of these memorable Augustan versions of a Roman ideal.

Johnson knew as well as did Pope that a poet's fictional

representation "gives my breast a thousand pains, / Can make me feel each Passion that he feigns" (*Epistle II, i, 343). Rambler* 4 and 60, *Idler* 84, discussions of the illusion of reality in Shakespeare, the almost Coleridgean response to the sylph machinery in Pope's *Rape of the Lock,* and many more instances indicate remarkable sophistication on Johnson's part about the function of artistic illusion. By associating Levet with a long tradition of concrete embodiments of the idea of the Good Man, he installs Levet once and for all in the membership of similar literary types. There, in a tradition, Levet triumphs against time and mortality, ever to be re-created in the reader's imaginative response to a moral ideal fixed in the permanence of form. It is not so much that Johnson distrusted fictions and the imagination, as is often claimed, but that he respected the inherent oppositions between art and life, time and permanence, reality and illusion — and treated them as oppositions. As Jean Hagstrum has put it, in describing Johnson's conception of imitation: "One contemplates art and remembers nature; simultaneously but inversely one remembers nature and contemplates art."[15]

This interplay between the idea of art as a defense against time and the fact of mortality leads to a recognition that art is finally no match for the human experience of time, a point fully expressed in the extended image of Levet (representing all of mankind) as a prisoner in a mine:

> Condemn'd to hope's delusive mine,
>   As on we toil from day to day. . . .
> In misery's darkest caverns known,
>   His useful care was ever nigh. . . .
> Death broke at once the vital chain,
>   And free'd his soul the nearest way. (1-2, 17-18, 35-36)

This familiar idea of the inevitability of human disappointment persists throughout Johnson's writings. "Hope," according to Johnson in *Rambler* 67, "is necessary in every condition." But as Arieh Sachs points out, "earthly hope . . . is fundamentally absurd" for Johnson, born out of a combination of "the vacuity

15. *Samuel Johnson's Literary Criticism* (Chicago: University of Chicago Press, 1952), p. 166.

of life" (Mrs. Thrale's phrase) and the dangerously prevalent imagination.[16]

A contrast is drawn, however, between feelings of despair and disappointment caused by these delusions of earthly happiness and by the futile toiling amidst shattered hopes, and the idea of Levet's "useful care" and ability to provide "social comforts" in such a world. The speaker carefully exempts from his indictment Levet's meaningful "toil," which he views as singularly redeeming and rewarding despite man's general predicament:

> Death broke at once the vital chain,
> And free'd his soul the nearest way. (35-36)

The diction reflects strong religious faith and confidence in the promise of Christian transcendence, the final dispensation of human history. But Levet's ironic achievement of freedom in death (based on Johnson's Christian orthodoxy) contrasts with the speaker's own deepening despair, culminating in full acceptance of the irrevocable fact of death. Against these contrasting patterns of movement exists the speaker-poet's positive achievement of a moment of reality redeemed from time through imaginative idealization and artistic transformation. As a creation of the speaker, this image becomes the artistic counterpart to Levet's timeless realm. The reality of despair, loss, and death in a context of time is challenged in the poem, as we have seen, by man's capacity to imagine and to force into some kind of coherent meaning the disparate actualities of a time-disordered world. Krieger brilliantly describes these complex effects of engagement and disengagement: "Levet provides the pattern of existence (indeed existence abstracted into pure pattern) which permits the self-consciousness, the dramatic discontinuities in all experience outside [Johnson's] own to be momentarily reduced to order."[16a] Illusory as this artistic representation of reality may ultimately be, it enables the speaker to win a measure of self-understanding and enjoy a momentary release from the tragic necessity of time.

Augustan poetry, by all reports, is supposed to be concerned with general truths, not self-expressive or concerned with

---

16. *Passionate Intelligence: Imagination and Reason in the Work of Samuel Johnson* (Baltimore: Johns Hopkins Press, 1967), p. 111.

16a. *The Classic Vision,* p. 144.

the inner workings of the private consciousness. But Augustan elegy, on the contrary, is a dramatization of a speaker's way of facing and coping with the inexorable flux of time. Even the moral conviction and Christian faith expressed in the elegy are finally products of the elegiac imagination. Through artifice, the craft of poetry itself, this moment of grief and praise is fixed within the continuum of time, and the act of elegizing transforms the actual fact of death into a more tractable poetic death. Thus the illusion created represents the speaker's attempt to shape a poetic world as a defense against time and mortality. But the occasion of elegy nevertheless re-emphasizes the realities of time which the poem as verbal artifact attempts to invalidate.

The structure of Johnson's elegy, then, mirrors these familiar oppositions between imagination and reality, art and life, permanence and time informing Augustan elegy. Johnson's maintenance of this basic dialectic throughout the poem explains the presence of the last two stanzas, which have had their detractors:

> The busy day, the peaceful night,
> Unfelt, uncounted, glided by;
> His frame was firm, his powers were bright,
> Tho' now his eightieth year was nigh.

> Then with no throbbing fiery pain,
> No cold gradations of decay,
> Death broke at once the vital chain,
> And free'd his soul the nearest way. (29-36)

Bertrand Bronson, for example, contends that they fail *because* they are specific, and that when Johnson reverts to generalizations about common experience, his characteristically weighty tone is infinitely more successful.[17] But Johnson is simply sustaining the elegiac ambivalence felt in the poem even in these final stanzas. For they are totally conventional and expected in two obvious ways: they complete the traditional organizing design — especially operative in pastoral elegy — which takes the victim from mortality to immortality through apotheosis. They also provide the equally traditional circumscription of imaginative idealizations characteristic of Augustan elegy. Much like Milton's deliberate change of perspective at the end of *Lycidas,* where the speaker

17. "Personification Reconsidered," p. 150.

shifts his focus away from the fictional day comprising the meditation to the everyday realities of a shepherd's life, Johnson changes the perspective from imaginative idealizations of praise to the mundane details of Levet's "eightieth year" and moment of death. As with Milton's speaker the living must necessarily go on living in the actual world. Johnson resignedly views Levet's death here as a natural and inevitable occurrence in a time-ridden world.

"On the Death of Dr. Robert Levet" is surely sincere by any standards invoked, but it is hardly because Johnson avoids art and artifice and instead resorts to poetry of statement and direct expression of grief. The poem demonstrates, rather, what David Perkins helpfully calls the "drama of sincerity, a poetry that displays or implies the struggle, and the cost, when a man tries to be honest with himself and completely faithful to his experience."[18] This faithfulness to experience exhibited in the poem involves more than Johnsonian concentration and moral weightiness. We feel, as always with Johnson, the massive personality and moral consciousness behind the materials of art. But the formal ordering of experience, as F. R. Leavis rightly insists, depends on "a constant presence of critical intelligence [that] makes Johnson's most solemn moralizing quite unlike anything of the next century."[19] This "critical intelligence" accounts for the dignity of tone and integrity of illusion which characterize Johnson's rendering of a complex interplay of elegiac attitudes toward art and time.

18. *Wordsworth and the Poetry of Sincerity* (Cambridge, Massachusetts: Belknap Press, 1964), p. 2. In his excellent study of sincerity in Wordsworth's poetry, Perkins shows that not until the later eighteenth century were a poet's personal beliefs, honesty of feeling, or emotional sympathy at issue: no one, he points out, would have worried whether or not Pope, for instance, was "sincere" in our modern sense of expressing genuine personal feeling.

19. *Revaluation: Tradition and Development in English Poetry* (London: Chatto and Windus, 1949), p. 119.

To the Memory of Mr. Oldham

FAREWEL, too little and too lately known,
Whom I began to think and call my own;
For sure our Souls were near ally'd; and thine
Cast in the same Poetick mould with mine.
One common Note on either Lyre did strike,   5
And Knaves and Fools we both abhorr'd alike:
To the same Goal did both our Studies drive,
The last set out the soonest did arrive.
Thus *Nisus* fell upon the slippery place,
While his young Friend perform'd and won the Race.   10
O early ripe! to thy abundant store
What could advancing Age have added more?
It might (what Nature never gives the young)
Have taught the numbers of thy native Tongue.
But Satyr needs not those, and Wit will shine   15
Through the harsh cadence of a rugged line.
A noble Error, and but seldom made,
And Poets are by too much force betray'd.
Thy generous fruits, though gather'd ere their prime
Still shew'd a quickness; and maturing time   20
But mellows what we write to the dull sweets of Rime.
Once more, hail and farewel; farewel thou young,
But ah too short, *Marcellus* of our Tongue;
Thy Brows with Ivy, and with Laurels bound;
But Fate and gloomy Night encompass thee around.   25

Elegy to the Memory of an Unfortunate Lady

What beck'ning ghost, along the moonlight shade
Invites my step, and points to yonder glade?

'Tis she! — but why that bleeding bosom gor'd,
Why dimly gleams the visionary sword?
Oh ever beauteous, ever friendly! tell, 5
Is it, in heav'n, a crime to love too well?
To bear too tender, or too firm a heart,
To act a Lover's or a *Roman's* part?
Is there no bright reversion in the sky,
For those who greatly think, or bravely die? 10
      Why bade ye else, ye Pow'rs! her soul aspire
Above the vulgar flight of low desire?
Ambition first sprung from your blest abodes;
The glorious fault of Angels and of Gods:
Thence to their Images on earth it flows, 15
And in the breasts of Kings and Heroes glows!
Most souls, 'tis true, but peep out once an age,
Dull sullen pris'ners in the body's cage:
Dim lights of life that burn a length of years,
Useless, unseen, as lamps in sepulchres; 20
Like Eastern Kings a lazy state they keep,
And close confin'd to their own palace sleep.
      From these perhaps (ere nature bade her die)
Fate snatch'd her early to the pitying sky.
As into air the purer spirits flow, 25
And sep'rate from their kindred dregs below;
So flew the soul to its congenial place,
Nor left one virtue to redeem her Race.
      But thou, false guardian of a charge too good,
Thou, mean deserter of thy brother's blood! 30
See on these ruby lips the trembling breath,
These cheeks, now fading at the blast of death:
Cold in that breast which warm'd the world before,
And those love-darting eyes must roll no more.
Thus, if eternal justice rules the ball, 35
Thus shall your wives, and thus your children fall:
On all the line a sudden vengeance waits,
And frequent herses shall besiege your gates.
There passengers shall stand, and pointing say,

(While the long fun'rals blacken all the way) 40
Lo these were they, whose souls the Furies steel'd,
And curs'd with hearts unknowing how to yield.
Thus unlamented pass the proud away,
The gaze of fools, and pageant of a day!
So perish all, whose breast ne'er learn'd to glow 45
For others' good, or melt at others' woe.
      What can atone (oh ever-injur'd shade!)
Thy fate unpity'd, and thy rites unpaid?
No friend's complaint, no kind domestic tear
Pleas'd thy pale ghost, or grac'd thy mournful bier; 50
By foreign hands thy dying eyes were clos'd,
By foreign hands thy decent limbs compos'd,
By foreign hands thy humble grave adorn'd,
By strangers honour'd, and by strangers mourn'd!
What tho' no friends in sable weeds appear, 55
Grieve for an hour, perhaps, then mourn a year,
And bear about the mockery of woe
To midnight dances and the publick show?
What tho' no weeping Loves thy ashes grace,
Nor polish'd marble emulate thy face? 60
What tho' no sacred earth allow thee room,
Nor hallow'd dirge be mutter'd o'er thy tomb?
Yet shall thy grave with rising flow'rs be drest,
And the green turf lie lightly on thy breast:
There shall the morn her earliest tears bestow; 65
There the first roses of the year shall blow;
While Angels with their silver wings o'ershade
The ground, now sacred by thy reliques made.
      So peaceful rests, without a stone, a name,
What once had beauty, titles, wealth, and fame. 70
How lov'd, how honour'd once, avails thee not,
To whom related, or by whom begot;
A heap of dust alone remains of thee;
'Tis all thou art, and all the proud shall be!
      Poets themselves must fall, like those they sung; 75
Deaf the prais'd ear, and mute the tuneful tongue.

Ev'n he, whose soul now melts in mournful lays,
Shall shortly want the gen'rous tear he pays;
Then from his closing eyes thy form shall part,
And the last pang shall tear thee from his heart,   80
Life's idle business at one gasp be o'er,
The Muse forgot, and thou belov'd no more!

An Epitaph.

Stet quicunque volet potens

Aulae culmine lubrico, & c. Senec.

INTERR'D beneath this Marble Stone,
Lie Saunt'ring JACK, and Idle JOAN.
While rolling Threescore Years and One
Did round this Globe their Courses run;
If Human Things went Ill or Well;   5
If changing Empires rose or fell;
The Morning past, the Evening came,
And found this Couple still the same.
They Walk'd and Eat, good Folks: What then?
Why then They Walk'd and Eat again: 10
They soundly slept the Night away:
They did just Nothing all the Day:
And having bury'd Children Four,
Wou'd not take Pains to try for more.
Nor Sister either had, nor Brother: 15
They seem'd just Tally'd for each other.

     Their Moral and Oeconomy
Most perfectly They made agree:
Each Virtue kept it's proper Bound,
Nor Trespass'd on the other's Ground.   20
Nor Fame, nor Censure They regarded:
They neither Punish'd, nor Rewarded.
He car'd not what the Footmen did:
Her Maids She neither prais'd, nor chid:

So ev'ry Servant took his Course;   25
And bad at First, They all grew worse.
Slothful Disorder fill'd His Stable;
And sluttish Plenty deck'd Her Table.
Their Beer was strong; Their Wine was *Port;*
Their Meal was large; Their Grace was short.   30
They gave the Poor the Remnant-meat,
Just when it grew not fit to eat.

  They paid the Church and Parish-Rate;
And took, but read not the Receit:
For which They claim'd their *Sunday's* Due,   35
Of slumb'ring in an upper Pew.

  No Man's Defects sought They to know;
So never made Themselves a Foe.
No Man's good Deeds did They commend;
So never rais'd Themselves a Friend.   40
Nor cherish'd They Relations poor:
That might decrease Their present Store:
Nor Barn nor House did they repair;
That might oblige their future Heir.

  They neither Added, nor Confounded: 45
They neither Wanted, nor Abounded.
Each *Christmas* They Accompts did clear;
And wound their Bottom round the Year.
Nor Tear, nor Smile did they imploy
At News of Public Grief, or Joy.   50
When Bells were Rung, and Bonfires made;
If ask'd, They ne'er deny'd their Aid:
Their Jugg was to the Ringers carry'd;
Who ever either Dy'd, or Marry'd.
Their Billet at the Fire was found;   55
Who ever was Depos'd, or Crown'd.

  Nor Good, nor Bad, nor Fools, nor Wise;
They wou'd not learn, nor cou'd advise:
Without Love, Hatred, Joy, or Fear,

They led — a kind of — as it were: 60
Nor Wish'd, nor Car'd, nor Laugh'd, nor Cry'd:
And so They liv'd; and so They dy'd.

Verses on the Death of Dr. Swift

As *Rochefoucault* his Maxims drew
From Nature, I believe 'em true:
They argue no corrupted Mind
In him; the Fault is in Mankind.

This Maxim more than all the rest   5
Is thought too base for human Breast;
"In all Distresses of our Friends
"We first consult our private Ends,
"While Nature kindly bent to ease us,
"Points out some Circumstance to please us.   10

If this perhaps your Patience move
Let Reason and Experience prove.

We all behold with envious Eyes,
Our *Equal* rais'd above our *Size*;
Who wou'd not at a crowded Show,   15
Stand high himself, keep others low?
I love my Friend as well as you,
But would not have him stop my View;
Then let him have the higher Post;
I ask but for an Inch at most.   20

If in a Battle you should find,
One, whom you love of all Mankind,
Had some heroick Action done,
A Champion kill'd, or Trophy won;
Rather than thus be over-topt,   25
Would you not wish his Lawrels cropt?

Dear honest *Ned* is in the Gout,
Lies rackt with Pain, and you without:

How patiently you hear him groan!
How glad the Case is not your own!   30

    What Poet would not grieve to see,
His Brethren write as well as he?
But rather than they should excel,
He'd wish his Rivals all in Hell.

    Her End when Emulation misses,   35
She turns to Envy, Stings and Hisses:
The strongest Friendship yields to Pride,
Unless the Odds be on our Side.

    Vain human Kind! Fantastick Race!
Thy various Follies, who can trace?   40
Self-love, Ambition, Envy, Pride,
Their Empire in our Hearts divide:
Give others Riches, Power, and Station,
'Tis all on me an Usurpation.
I have no Title to aspire;   45
Yet, when you sink, I seem the higher.
In POPE, I cannot read a Line,
But with a Sigh, I wish it mine:
When he can in one Couplet fix
More Sense than I can do in Six: 50
It gives me such a jealous Fit,
I cry, Pox take him, and his Wit.

    Why must I be outdone by GAY,
In my own hum'rous biting Way?

    ARBUTHNOT is no more my Friend,   55
Who dares to Irony pretend;
Which I was born to introduce,
Refin'd it first, and shew'd its Use.

    St. JOHN, as well as PULTNEY knows,
That I had some repute for Prose;   60
And till they drove me out of Date,

Could maul a Minister of State:
If they have mortify'd my Pride,
And made me throw my Pen aside;
If with such Talents Heav'n hath blest'em   65
Have I not Reason to detest 'em?

     To all my Foes, dear Fortune, send
Thy Gifts, but never to my Friend:
I tamely can endure the first,
But, this with Envy makes me burst.   70

     Thus much may serve by way of Proem,
Proceed we therefore to our Poem.

     The Time is not remote when I
Must by the Course of Nature dye:
When I foresee my special Friends,   75
Will try to find their private Ends:
Tho' it is hardly understood,
Which way my Death can do them good;
Yet, thus methinks, I hear 'em speak;
See, how the Dean begins to break: 80
Poor Gentleman, he droops apace,
You plainly find it in his Face:
That old Vertigo in his Head,
Will never leave him, till he's dead:
Besides, his Memory decays,   85
He recollects not what he says;
He cannot call his Friends to Mind;
Forgets the Place where last he din'd:
Plyes you with Stories o'er and o'er,
He told them fifty Times before.   90
How does he fancy we can sit,
To hear his out-of-fashion'd Wit?
But he takes up with Younger Fokes,
Who for his Wine will bear his Jokes:
Faith, he must make his Stories shorter,   95
Or Change his Comrades once a Quarter:

In half the Time, he talks them round;
There must another Sett be found.

For Poetry, he's past his Prime,
He takes an Hour to find a Rhime: 100
His Fire is out, his Wit decay'd,
His Fancy sunk, his Muse a Jade.
I'd have him throw away his Pen;
But there's no talking to some Men.

And, then their Tenderness appears,   105
By adding largely to my Years:
"He's older than he would be reckon'd,
"And well remembers *Charles* the Second.

"He hardly drinks a Pint of Wine;
"And that, I doubt, is no good Sign.   110
"His Stomach too begins to fail:
"Last Year we thought him strong and hale;
"But now, he's quite another Thing;
"I wish he may hold out till Spring.

Then hug themselves, and reason thus;   115
"It is not yet so bad with us."

In such a Case they talk in Tropes,
And, by their Fears express their Hopes;
Some great Misfortune to portend,
No Enemy can match a Friend;   120
With all the Kindness they profess,
The Merit of a lucky Guess,
(When daily Howd'y's come of Course,
And Servants answer; *Worse and Worse*)
Wou'd please 'em better than to tell,   125
That, GOD be prais'd, the Dean is well.
Then he who prophecy'd the best,
Approves his Foresight to the rest:
"You know, I always fear'd the worst,
"And often told you so at first:"   130

He'd rather chuse that I should dye,
Than his Prediction prove a Lye.
Not one foretels I shall recover;
But, all agree, to give me over.

Yet shou'd some Neighbour feel a Pain,   135
Just in the Parts, where I complain;
How many a Message would he send?
What hearty Prayers that I should mend?
Enquire what Regimen I kept;
What gave me Ease, and how I slept?   140
And more lament, when I was dead,
Then all the Sniv'llers round my Bed.

My good Companions, never fear,
For though you may mistake a Year;
Though your Prognosticks run too fast,   145
They must be verify'd at last.

"Behold the fatal Day arrive!
"How is the Dean? He's just alive.
"Now the departing Prayer is read:
"He hardly breathes. The Dean is dead.   150
"Before the Passing-Bell begun,
"The News thro' half the Town has run.
"O, may we all for Death prepare!
"What has he left? And who's his Heir?
"I know no more than what the News is,   155
" 'Tis all bequeath'd to public Uses.
"To public Use! A perfect Whim!
"What had the Publick done for him!
"Meer Envy, Avarice, and Pride!
He gave it all: — But first he dy'd.   160
"And had the Dean, in all the Nation,
"No worthy Friend, no poor Relation?
"So ready to do Strangers good,
"Forgetting his own Flesh and Blood?

    Now Grub-Street Wits are all employ'd;   165
With Elegies, the Town is cloy'd:
Some Paragraph in ev'ry Paper,
To *curse* the *Dean,* or *bless* the *Drapier.*

    The Doctors tender of their Fame,
Wisely on me lay all the Blame: 170
"We must confess his Case was nice;
"But he would never take Advice:
"Had he been rul'd, for ought appears,
"He might have liv'd these Twenty Years:
"For when we open'd him we found,   175
"That all his vital Parts were sound.

    From *Dublin* soon to *London* spread,
'Tis told at Court, The Dean is dead.

    Kind Lady *Suffolk* in the Spleen,
Runs laughing up to tell the Queen.   180
The Queen, so Gracious, Mild, and Good,
Cries, "Is he gone? 'Tis time he shou'd.
"He's dead you say; why let him rot;
"I'm glad the Medals were forgot.
"I promis'd them, I own; but when?   185
"I only was the Princess then;
"But now as Consort of the King,
"You know 'tis quite a different Thing.

    Now, *Chartres* at Sir *Robert's* Levee,
Tells, with a Sneer, the Tidings heavy: 190
"Why, is he dead without his Shoes?
(Cries *Bob*) "I'm sorry for the News;
Oh, were the Wretch but living still,
And in his Place my good Friend *Will*;
Or, had a Mitre on his Head   195
Provided *Bolingbroke* were dead.

    Now *Curl* his Shop from Rubbish drains;

Three genuine Tomes of *Swift's* Remains.
And then to make them pass the glibber,
Revis'd by *Tibbalds, Moore, and Cibber.*   200
He'll treat me as he does my Betters.
Publish my Will, my Life, my Letters.
Revive the Libels born to dye;
Which POPE must bear, as well as I.

Here shift the Scene, to represent   205
How those I love, my Death lament.
Poor POPE will grieve a Month; and GAY
A Week; and ARBUTHNOTT a Day.

St. John himself will scarce forbear,
To bite his Pen, and drop a Tear.   210
The rest will give a Shrug and cry,
I'm sorry; but we all must dye.
Indifference clad in Wisdom's Guise,
All Fortitude of Mind supplies:
For how can stony Bowels melt,   215
In those who never Pity felt;
When *We* are lash'd, *They* kiss the Rod;
Resigning to the Will of God.

The Fools, my Juniors by a Year,
Are tortur'd with Suspence and Fear.   220
Who wisely thought my Age a Screen,
When Death approach'd, to stand between:
The Screen remov'd, their Hearts are trembling,
They mourn for me without dissembling.

My female Friends, whose tender Hearts   225
Have better learn'd to act their Parts.
Receive the News in *doleful Dumps,*
"The Dean is dead, (*and what is Trumps?*)
"Then Lord have Mercy on his Soul.
"(Ladies I'll venture for the *Vole.*)   230
"Six Deans they say must bear the Pall.
"(I wish I knew what *King* to call.)

"Madam, your Husband will attend
"The Funeral of so good a Friend.
"No Madam, 'tis a shocking Sight,   235
"And he's engag'd To-morrow Night!
"My Lady *Club* wou'd take it ill,
"If he shou'd fail her at *Quadrill.*
"He lov'd the Dean. (*I lead a Heart.*)
"But dearest Friends, they say, must part. 240
"His Time was come, he ran his Race;
"We hope he's in a better Place.

  Why do we grieve that Friends should dye?
No Loss more easy to supply.
One Year is past; a different Scene;   245
No further mention of the Dean;
Who now, alas, no more is mist,
Than if he never did exist.
Where's now this Fav'rite of *Apollo?*
Departed; *and his Works must follow:* 250
Must undergo the common Fate;
His Kind of Wit is out of Date.
Some Country Squire to *Lintot* goes,
Enquires for SWIFT in Verse and Prose: 255
Says *Lintot,* "I have heard the Name:
"He dy'd a Year ago." "The same."
"Sir you may find them in *Duck-lane:*
"I sent them with a Load of Books,
"Last *Monday* to the Pastry-cooks.   260
"To fancy they cou'd live a Year!
"I find you're but a Stranger here.
"The Dean was famous in his Time;
"And had a Kind of Knack at Rhyme:
"His way of Writing now is past;   265
"The Town hath got a better Taste:
"I keep no antiquated Stuff;
"But, spick and span I have enough.
"Pray, do but give me leave to shew 'em;

"Here's *Colley Cibber's* Birth-day Poem.   270
"This Ode you never yet have seen,
"By *Stephen Duck,* upon the Queen.
"Then, here's a Letter finely penn'd
"Against the *Craftsman* and his Friend;
"It clearly shews that all Reflection   275
"On Ministers, is disaffection.
"Next, here's Sir *Robert's* Vindication,
"And Mr. *Henly's* last Oration:
"The Hawkers have not got 'em yet,
"Your Honour please to buy a Set?   280

      "Here's *Wolston's* Tracts, the twelfth Edition;
" 'Tis read by ev'ry Politician:
"The Country Members, when in Town,
"To all their Boroughs send them down:
"You never met a Thing so smart;   285
"The Courtiers have them all by Heart:
"Those Maids of Honour (who can read)
"Are taught to use them for their Creed.
"The Rev'rend Author's good Intention,
"Hath been rewarded with a Pension: 290
"He doth an Honour to his Gown,
"By bravely running *Priest-craft* down:
"He shews, as sure as GOD's in *Gloc'ster,*
"That *Jesus* was a Grand Impostor:
"That all his Miracles were Cheats,   295
"Perform'd as Juglers do their Feats:
"The Church had never such a Writer:
"A Shame, he hath not got a Mitre!

      Suppose me dead; and then suppose
A Club assembled at the *Rose*;   300
Where from Discourse of this and that,
I grow the Subject of their Chat:
And, while they toss my Name about,
With Favour some, and some without;
One quite indiff'rent in the Cause,   305

My Character impartial draws:

"The Dean, if we believe Report,
"Was never ill receiv'd at Court:
"As for his Works in Verse and Prose,
"I own my self no Judge of those: 310
"Nor, can I tell what Criticks thought 'em;
"But, this I know, all People bought 'em;
"As with a moral View design'd
"To cure the Vices of Mankind:
"His Vein, ironically grave,   315
"Expos'd the Fool, and lash'd the Knave:
"To steal a Hint was never known,
"But what he writ was all his own.

"He never thought an Honour done him,
"Because a Duke was proud to own him: 320
"Would rather slip aside, and chuse
"To talk with Wits in dirty Shoes:
"Despis'd the Fools with Stars and Garters,
"So often seen caressing *Chartres:*
"He never courted Men in Station,   325
"Nor Persons had in Admiration;
"Of no Man's Greatness was afraid,
"Because he sought for no Man's Aid.
"Though trusted long in great Affairs,
"He gave himself no haughty Airs: 330
"Without regarding private Ends,
"Spent all his Credit for his Friends:
"And only chose the Wise and Good;
"No Flatt'rers; no Allies in Blood;
"But succour'd Virtue in Distress,   335
"And seldom fail'd of good Success;
"As Numbers in their Hearts must own,
"Who, but for him, had been unknown.

"With Princes kept a due Decorum,
"But never stood in Awe before 'em: 340

"He follow'd *David's* Lesson just,
"*In Princes never put thy Trust.*
"And, would you make him truly sower;
"Provoke him with *a slave in Power*:
"The *Irish* Senate, if you nam'd,   345
"With what Impatience he declaim'd!
"Fair LIBERTY was all his Cry;
"For her he stood prepar'd to die;
"For her he boldly stood alone;
"For her he oft expos'd his own.   350
"Two Kingdoms, just as Faction led,
"Had set a Price upon his Head;
"But, not a Traytor cou'd be found,
"To sell him for Six Hundred Pound.

    "Had he but spar'd his Tongue and Pen,   355
"He might have rose like other Men:
"But, Power was never in his Thought;
"And, Wealth he valu'd not a Groat:
"Ingratitude he often found,
"And pity'd those who meant the Wound: 360
"But, kept the Tenor of his Mind,
"To merit well of human Kind:
"Nor made a Sacrifice of those
"Who still were true, to please his Foes.
"He labour'd many a fruitless Hour   365
"To reconcile his Friends in Power;
"Saw Mischief by a Faction brewing,
"While they pursu'd each others Ruin.
"But, finding vain was all his Care,
"He left the Court in meer Despair.   370

    "And, oh! how short are human Schemes!
"Here ended all our golden Dreams.
"What ST. JOHN's Skill in State Affairs,
"What ORMOND's *Valour,* OXFORD's Cares,
"To save their sinking Country lent,   375
"Was all destroy'd by one Event.

"Too soon that precious Life was ended,
"On which alone, our Weal depended.
"When up a dangerous Faction starts,
"With Wrath and Vengeance in their Hearts: 380
"By solemn League and Cov'nant bound,
"To ruin, slaughter, and confound;
"To turn Religion to a Fable,
"And make the Government a *Babel*:
"Pervert the Law, disgrace the Gown, 385
"Corrupt the Senate, rob the Crown;
"To sacrifice old *England*"s Glory,
"And make her infamous in Story.
"When such a Tempest shook the Land,
"How could unguarded Virtue stand? 390

"With Horror, Grief, Despair the Dean
"Beheld the dire destructive Scene:
"His Friends in Exile, or the Tower,
"Himself within the Frown of Power;
"Pursu'd by base envenom'd Pens, 395
"Far to the Land of Slaves and Fens;
"A servile Race in Folly nurs'd,
"Who truckle most, when treated worst.

"By Innocence and Resolution,
"He bore continual Persecution; 400
"While Numbers to Preferment rose;
"Whose Merits were, to be his Foes.
"When, *ev'n his own familiar Friends*
"Intent upon their private Ends;
"Like Renegadoes now he feels, 405
"Against him lifting up their Heels.

"The Dean did by his Pen defeat
"An infamous destructive Cheat.
"Taught Fools their Int'rest how to know;
"And gave them Arms to ward the Blow. 410
"Envy hath own'd it was his doing,

"To save that helpless Land from Ruin,
"While they who at the Steerage stood,
"And reapt the Profit, sought his Blood.

"To save them from their evil Fate,   415
"In him was held a Crime of State.
"A wicked Monster on the Bench,
"Whose Fury Blood could never quench;
"As vile and profligate a Villain,
"As modern *Scroggs,* or old *Tressilian*;   420
"Who long all Justice had discarded,
"*Nor fear'd he GOD, nor Man regarded*;
"Vow'd on the Dean his Rage to vent,
"And make him of his Zeal repent;
"But Heav'n his Innocence defends,   425
"The grateful People stand his Friends:
"Not Strains of Law, nor Judges Frown,
"Nor Topicks brought to please the Crown,
"Nor Witness hir'd, nor Jury pick'd,
"Prevail to bring him in convict.   430

"In Exile with a steady Heart,
"He spent his Life's declining Part;
"Where, Folly, Pride and Faction sway,
"Remote from ST. JOHN, POPE, and GAY.

"His Friendship there to few confin'd,   435
"Were always of the midling Kind:
"No Fools of Rank, a mungril Breed,
"Who fain would pass for Lords indeed:
"Where Titles give no Right or Power,
"And Peerage is a wither'd Flower.   440
"He would have held it a Disgrace,
"If such a Wretch had known his Face.
"On Rural Squires, that Kingdom's Bane,
"He vented oft his Wrath in vain:
"Biennial Squires, to Market brought;   445
"Who sell their Souls and Votes for Naught;

"The Nation stript go joyful back,
"To rob the Church, their Tenants rack,
"Go Snacks with Thieves and Rapparees,
"And, keep the Peace, to pick up Fees: 450
"In every Jobb to have a Share,
"A Jayl or Barrack to repair;
"And turn the Tax for publick Roads
"Commodious to their own Abodes.

    "Perhaps I may allow, the Dean 455
"Had too much Satyr in his Vein;
"And seem'd determin'd not to starve it,
"Because no Age could more deserve it.
"Yet, Malice never was his Aim;
"He lash'd the Vice but spar'd the Name. 460
"No Individual could resent,
"Where Thousands equally were meant.
"His Satyr points at no Defect,
"But what all Mortals may correct;
"For he abhorr'd that senseless Tribe, 465
"Who call it Humour when they jibe:
"He spar'd a Hump or crooked Nose,
"Whose Owners set not up for Beaux.
"True genuine Dulness mov'd his Pity,
"Unless it offer'd to be witty. 470
"Those, who their Ignorance confess'd,
"He ne'er offended with a Jest;
"But laugh'd to hear an Idiot quote,
"A Verse from *Horace,* learn'd by Rote.
    "He knew an hundred pleasant Stories, 475
"With all the Turns of *Whigs* and *Tories*:
"Was chearful to his dying Day,
"And Friends would let him have his Way.

    "He gave the little Wealth he had,
"To build a House for Fools and Mad: 480
"And shew'd by one satyric Touch,
"No Nation wanted it so much:

"That Kingdom he hath left his Debtor,
"I wish it soon may have a Better.

On the Death of Richard West

In vain to me the smileing Mornings shine,
And redning Phoebus lifts his golden Fire:
The Birds in vain their amorous Descant joyn;
Or chearful Fields resume their green Attire:
These Ears, alas! for other Notes repine, 5
A different Object do these Eyes require.
My lonely Anguish melts no Heart, but mine;
And in my Breast the imperfect Joys expire.
Yet Morning smiles the busy Race to chear,
And new-born Pleasure brings to happier Men: 10
The Fields to all their wonted Tribute bear:
To warm their little Loves the Birds complain:
I fruitless mourn to him, that cannot hear,
And weep the more, because I weep in vain.

On the Death of Dr. Robert Levet

Condemn'd to hope's delusive mine,
    As on we toil from day to day,
By sudden blasts, or slow decline,
    Our social comforts drop away.

Well tried through many a varying year, 5
    See LEVET to the grave descend;
Officious, innocent, sincere,
    Of ev'ry friendless name the friend.

Yet still he fills affection's eye,
    Obscurely wise, and coarsely kind; 10
Nor, letter'd arrogance, deny
    Thy praise to merit unrefin'd.

When fainting nature call'd for aid,
    And hov'ring death prepar'd the blow,

His vig'rous remedy display'd   15
    The power of art without the show.

In misery's darkest caverns known,
    His useful care was ever nigh,
Where hopeless anguish pour'd his groan,
    And lonely want retir'd to die.   20

No summons mock'd by chill delay,
    No petty gain disdain'd by pride,
The modest wants of ev'ry day
    The toil of ev'ry day supplied.

His virtues walk'd their narrow round,   25
    Nor made a pause, nor left a void;
And sure th'Eternal Master found
    The single talent well employ'd.

The busy day, the peaceful night,
    Unfelt, uncounted, glided by;   30
His frame was firm, his powers were bright,
    Tho' now his eightieth year was nigh.

Then with no throbbing fiery pain,
    No cold gradations of decay,
Death broke at once the vital chain,   35
    And free'd his soul the nearest way.

INDEX

Page numbers in italics indicate discussions of authors and elegies

OTHER BOOKS AVAILABLE:

Haldeen Braddy: Hamlet's Wounded Name. 2nd enlarged edition by the author and with new introduction by James T. Bratcher. Amsterdam 1974. XV, 82 pp.   Hfl. 16,–

Sandy Cohen: Bernard Malamud and the Trial by Love. Amsterdam 1974. 132 pp. (Melville Studies in American Culture. Edited by Robert Brainard Pearsal, vol. 1)   Hfl. 18,–

Joseph Flibbert: Melville and the Art of Burlesque. Amsterdam 1974. 163 pp. (Melville Studies in American Culture. Edited by Robert Brainard Pearsall. Vol. 3)   Hfl. 30.–

Wallace Jackson: Immediacy: The Development of a Critical Concept from Addison to Coleridge. Amsterdam 1973. 129 pp.
Hfl. 25,–

E. Anthony James: Daniel Defoe's Many Voices. A Rhetorical Study of Prose Style and Literary Method. Amsterdam 1972. 269 pp.   Hfl. 48.–

John B. McKee: Literary Irony and the Literary Audience: Studies in the Victimization of the Reader in Augustan Fiction. Amsterdam 1974. 114 pp.   Hfl. 16,–

Brian O. Murdoch: The Recapitulated Fall. A Comparative Study in Mediaeval Literature. Amsterdam 1974. 207 pp. (Amsterdamer Publikationen zur Sprache und Literatur, herausgegeben von Cola Minis, Band 11)   Hfl. 35,–

Robert Brainard Pearsall: Rupert Brooke. The Man and Poet. Amsterdam 1974. 176 pp.   Hfl. 25,–

Robert Brainard Pearsall: The Life and Writings of Ernest Hemingway. Amsterdam 1973. 282 pp. (Melville Studies in American Culture. Edited by Robert Brainard Pearsall, vol. 2)
Hfl. 35.–

Karl Ludwig Pfeiffer: Sprachtheorie, Wissenschaftstheorie und das Problem der Textinterpretation. Untersuchungen am Beispiel des *New Criticism* und Paul Valéry. Amsterdam 1974, V, 429 S.   Hfl. 70.—

Rhetoric of the People. "Is there any better or equal hope in the world? ". Edited and with Introductions by Harold Barrett. Amsterdam 1974. 335 pp.

Stiff covers Hfl. 29,—
Buckram binding Hfl. 58.—

John E. Saveson: Joseph Conrad: The Making of a Moralist. Amsterdam 1972. 195 pp.   Hfl. 35,—

John E. Saveson: Conrad, the Later Moralist. Amsterdam 1974. 129 pp.   Hfl. 25,—

J. Richard Stracke: The Laud Herbal Glossary edited. Amsterdam 1974. 208 pp.   Hfl. 60.—

Studies in Interpretation. Edited by Esther M. Doyle and Virginia H. Floyd. Amsterdam 1972. 362 pp.   Hfl. 42,—

Marion A. Taylor: Bottom, Thou Art Translated. Political Allegory in *A Midsummer Night's Dream* and Related Literature. Amsterdam 1973. 253 pp.   Hfl. 35,—

Frederic Will: The Fact of Literature. Three Essays on Public Material. Amsterdam 1973. VIII, 215 pp.   Hfl. 35.—

EDITIONS RODOPI NV
KEIZERSGRACHT 302-304
AMSTERDAM — THE NETHERLANDS

STUDIES
IN INTERPRETATION

edited by

Virginia H. Floyd & Esther M. Doyle

Analytical

Towards a Definition of Hubris by Virginia H. Floyd, Professor of Speech and Director of Readers Theatre at The University of Arizona.

The Shape of Sound: Configurational Rime in the Poetry of Dylan Thomas, by Katharina Loesch, Associate Professor of Speech, University of Illinois at Chicago Circle.

Contiguity Figures: an Index to the Language-World Relationship in Auden's Poetry by Lea Gibbs Queener, Associate Professor of Speech and Director of Interpretation at Memphis State University.

Diagnosis and Dialectic by Roland Rude, Teacher of Interpretation and Drama at New Trier High School.

Critical

Poet on Stage by Esther M. Doyle, Dana Professor of English at Juniata College.

The Interpreter and the Structure of the Novel by Lilla A. Heston, Associate Professor of Interpretation, School of Speech, Northwestern University.

The Interpreter and Modern Fiction: Problems of Point of View and Structural Tensiveness by Joanna Hawkins Maclay, Assistant Professor of Speech at the University of Illinois, Urbana.

Imagery and the Interpreter by Joseph A. Wigley, Associate Professor of Speech at The Pennsylvania State University.

The Unspoken Word by Elizabeth Worrell. Formely Professor of Speech at Northeast Missouri State College. Visiting Professor at The University of Missouri.

Historical

Oral Interpretation at the Chautauqua Institution and the Chautauqua School of Expression, 1874-1900 by Dorothy Siedenburg Hadley, Professor of Drama at San Jose State College

Oral Interpretation as a Means of Instruction in Anglo-Saxon England by Patricia Hampton, Member of the English Department faculty at Columbia State College in Tennessee.

Art and Nature: The Mechanical School in England, 1761-1806 by Alethea Smith Mattingly, Professor of Speech, The University of Arizona.

Theoretical

Physical Actions and the Oral Interpreter by Leslie Irene Coger, Professor of Speech and Theatre at Southwest Missouri State College.

Poetry as Awareness of What? by Don Geiger, poet, critic, consulting editor in speech for Random House, Professor of Rhetoric at the University of California, Berkeley.

A Communication Model for Oral Interpretation by Paul Hunsinger, who has taught at several colleges, and universities including Occidental College, Northwestern University, and the Universities of Denver and Hawaii.

The Poem's Text as a Technique of Performance in Public Group Readings of Poetry by Chester C. Long, Professor of Speech and Theatre, University of Illinois at Chicago Circle.

Speaking Literature by Thomas O. Sloan, Professor of Rhetoric and chairman of the department at the University of California, Berkeley.

362 pp.

	Stiff covers:	Hfl. 42.—	US-$ 15.50
	Buckram binding:	Hfl. 60.—	US-$ 22.00

LC 72-93572

EDITIONS RODOPI N.V.
Keizersgracht 302-304
Amsterdam-C.